PREFACE

I have been an environmental gardener all my life and aim to use chemical treatments only when absolutely forced to resort to 'fire fighting'. During my amateur gardening career I have tried many so called 'alternative' means of cultivation based on everyday organic gardening.

The Moon plays an important part in our life on Earth. Almost everyone knows that it is the influence of the Moon that creates the forces that cause the sea to move backwards and forwards within the ocean basins and produce tides on the shores of the continents. To a lesser but more impressive extent this gravitational pull also works on the landmass of the continents and causes them to flex.

The art of astrology is based on the pressures of the Moon and the much more distant planets on our beings at the time of birth.

So, is it surprising that the Moon can also influence the growth of plants? When sown at the right time in the lunar cycle the seed has time to settle in its new home in the soil and then push upwards with the assistance of favourable energies. All through the life of the plant the Moon's energy has a cyclic effect on its growth. At some times of the month its energy is being suppressed whilst at others it is being drawn upwards. It is at this time that the plant is best harvested to get the most goodness out of it.

This book ranges far beyond the effects of the Moon in the gardener's year. It looks at the pull of the Moon on our very bodies and how it can be used beneficially for our own health and even to find the most appropriate time for a hair cut!

This book is a mine of information on all things connected with the Moon and gives an insight into the lunar effect on plants, humanity and the planet.

David Shaw

David has been an organic gardener for over 35 years and works with the Scottish Environment Protection Agency.

Calculating world times

Times throughout the book are given in **Greenwich Mean Time** (26 October to 29 March) or **British Summer Time** (30 March to 25 October), as appropriate. **For those in the United Kingdom and Ireland, all times given, both summer and winter, are those shown on your watches.** The number of hours to take off or add on for other countries appear in the table below:

COUNTRY	From 1/1 to 29/3 From 26/10 to 31/12	From 30/3 to 25/10
USA (New York), Canada (Ottawa)*	- 5h*	- 5h
Iceland, Morocco	0h	- 1h
Canary Islands, Ireland, Portugal	0h	0h
Australia (Sydney)	+ 9h	+ 9h
Austria, Belgium, Czech Republic, Denmark, France, Germany, Holland, Hungary, Italy, Luxembourg, Norway, Poland, Slovakia, Spain, Sweden, Switzerland, Tunisia	+ 1h	+ 1h
South Africa	+ 2h	+ 1h
Bulgaria, Finland, Greece, Romania, Turkey	+ 2h	+ 2h
New Zealand**	+ 13h	+ 11h
Japan	+ 9h	+ 8h

* **USA (New York) and Canada (Ottawa)** from 9/3 to 29/3 and from 26/10 to 1/11: - 4h
** **New Zealand** from 30/3 to 6/4 and from 29/9 to 25/10: + 12h

Using the calendar made easy

This diagram provides a clearer, simpler version of the information contained in the tear-out section. This information is a summary of our interpretation of the various lunar and planetary influences.

Descending Moon: the band descends and the line is yellow

Between the New Moon and the Full Moon, the Moon is waxing.

Ascending Moon: the band ascends and the line is green

Avoid the red zones and the symbol (—)

Harvesting band
★ Green stars = harvest aerial plant parts
☆ Yellow stars = harvest plant parts below ground

The more stars there are, the more suitable the day is for sowing or cultivating the crop represented by the symbols

Cultivation band
The colour of the stars corresponds to the different types of crop

fruit = ★
root = ★
flower = ★
leaf = ★

CONTENTS

UNDERSTANDING THE MOON

The waxing and waning Moon

This is one of the most familiar features of the Moon as viewed from the Earth. What we are seeing is the Moon's monthly orbit around the Earth, which starts with the New Moon and takes 29 days, 12 hours and 44 minutes. When new, the Moon is positioned exactly between the Earth and the Sun – thus, the illuminated area of its surface is not visible from Earth. This phase is represented on the diagram below by a black circle. As the Moon progresses on its orbit, it reflects a crescent of light that expands until it is seen from Earth as a luminous disc – the Full Moon. In this phase, the Moon is on the opposite side of the Earth to the Sun. From that point on, the illuminated area decreases until the Moon renews its orbit once more.

The waxing Moon

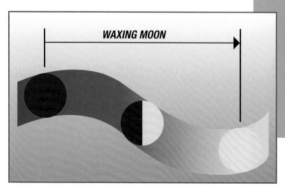

WAXING MOON

The Moon 'waxes' during the phase from New Moon to Full Moon – the illuminated area increases in size every day. On the calendar (pages 54–77), the colour of the blue band also becomes lighter as the Moon waxes.

In the night sky of the northern hemisphere, a quick glance will tell you if the Moon is waxing – the illuminated area is shaped like a crescent, which, if you were to add an imaginary line to the left of it, would resemble the letter 'p'. In the southern hemisphere, the illuminated area is also expanding but is seen the opposite way round, while in equatorial regions the crescent appears to be lying on its back.

This phase is indicated on the lunar calendar (pages 54–77) between the New Moon and the Full Moon.

Plants increase in vitality with moonlight and as the Full Moon approaches, their resistance to parasites and diseases increases. Fruits and vegetables harvested at this time store well and impart more vitality when eaten, while cut flowers last longer in a vase. Silage and mown hay are of better quality, compost is warmer and animals are less anxious when there are people around.

The waning Moon

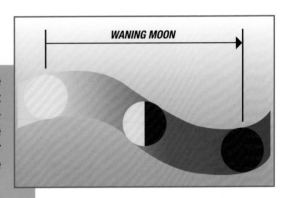

The Moon 'wanes' during the phase between the Full Moon and the next New Moon. Every night the illuminated area becomes smaller. On the calendar (pages 54–77), the colour of the blue band darkens as the Moon wanes.

In the sky of the northern hemisphere, the illuminated area of the waning Moon reverts to a crescent shape, but now if you were to add an imaginary line to the right of it, it would resemble the letter 'd'.

This phase lasts from the Full Moon to the next New Moon.

As the moonlight decreases, so does the vigour of plants, although their specific energy is increased – colours, scents and tastes are more perceptible during this phase, and nutritional and medicinal properties are more pronounced. However, it is more difficult to store harvested crops in their natural state and this phase is more suitable for preserving foods, making jams and bottling wine.

The ascending and descending Moon

Many people think that an ascending Moon is the same as a waxing one when in fact they are totally different. The Moon can, for example, wax and descend at the same time. The path of the ascending and descending Moon is similar to the progress of the Sun during the course of the year. In the northern hemisphere, the Sun rises in the south-east and sets in the south-west at the winter solstice, toward the end of December. The arc that it describes in the sky is very short and at noon it is very low on the southern horizon. The closer we are to the summer solstice at the end of June, the nearer to the north-east the Sun rises and the nearer to the north-west it sets. Its arc is much longer at this time and at noon the Sun is very close to its zenith. The sun is therefore ascending during the six months between the winter and summer solstices and descending during the six months between the summer and winter solstices. The Moon also ascends and descends, but over a period of 27 days, 7 hours and 43 minutes, known as the **periodic lunar cycle**. In the northern hemisphere, the Moon ascends in the sky and then descends again, while in the southern hemisphere the reverse takes place.

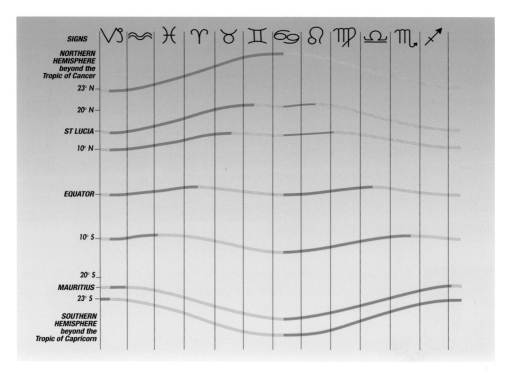

On the calendar on pages 54–77, the narrow coloured band beneath the date band shows the path of the ascending and descending Moon in the northern hemisphere as far as the Tropic of Cancer (to determine the path in the southern hemisphere, south of the Tropic of Capricorn, simply invert the colours). Between the two tropics, there is a regular pattern of inversion (see diagram above).

The influences of the ascending and descending Moon and Sun grow steadily weaker the nearer we get to the Equator. Beyond the tropics, the forces that result from such movements are linked with three factors: the ascending/descending Moon, the waxing/waning Moon and the tides (see page 14). Any of these factors can predominate – for example, in Europe, grafting is best done when the Moon is ascending. However, the nearer you are to the Equator, the more the influence of the ascending/descending Moon diminishes, while that of the two other factors increases. For instance, nearer the Equator it is more beneficial to graft plants when the Moon is waxing than when it is ascending.

In the northern and southern hemispheres, in regions beyond the tropics, the ascending/descending Moon has a very strong influence in certain areas of the lunar calendar. In equatorial regions, on the other hand, it is the waxing/waning Moon and the influences of the tide that have greater influence.

The Moon is ascending when, every night, its orbit is higher than the night before. Look at the Moon, ignoring the stars, for two consecutive nights to work out whether it is ascending or descending. On the first night, establish its position in the sky as accurately as possible. A little later on the following night, the Moon will pass through the same vertical once more. If it passes through at a greater height, you will know that it is ascending.

The ascending Moon

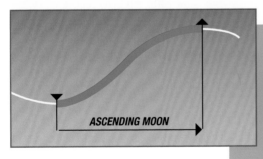

ASCENDING MOON

On the calendar (pages 54–77), the Moon is ascending when it travels from its lowest point (▼) to its highest (▲). This continual oscillation is shown in the illustration. When the curve rises, the Moon is ascending.

The fluids within plants rise and fall with the Moon. When the Moon is ascending, plants contain more sap so there is more activity in their aerial parts (those parts above ground). This is a good time, for example, to cut scions, **to graft plants and to harvest fruit** with a high juice content, as well as to collect sap from silver birches, etc. However, it is better to avoid pruning trees or cutting plants for drying at this time. Cutting lawns when the Moon is ascending tends to encourage plenty of growth; it is a good time to aerate them.

The descending Moon

On the calendar (pages 54–77), the Moon is descending when it travels from its highest point (▲) to its lowest (▼). When the curve falls, the Moon is descending.

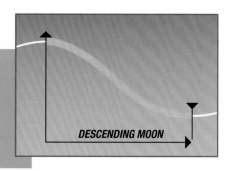

DESCENDING MOON

When the moon is descending, the flow of fluids in plants descends also and growth occurs mainly in the roots. This is a good time to harvest root crops or the aerial parts of a plant that you want to dry quickly, and also for pruning, pricking out, re-potting, ploughing, spreading compost or manure and cutting wood. The grass of lawns that are cut at this time forms stronger roots and anchors the soil better.

The distance from the Earth to the Moon

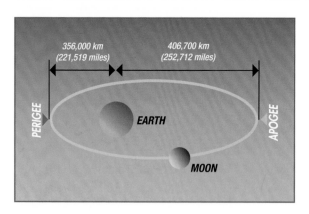

356,000 km (221,519 miles)

406,700 km (252,712 miles)

PERIGEE

EARTH

APOGEE

MOON

The Moon moves around an elliptical orbit, with the Earth as one of its foci. This means that the distance between the Earth and Moon is always changing. When the Moon is closest to the Earth, it is at its perigee, and when it is furthest away, it is at its apogee. The progress of the Moon from one perigee to the next is known as the anomalistic lunar cycle and takes 27 days, 13 hours and 18 minutes.

The Moon's effects on plants increases when it nears the Earth and its influence is, therefore, strongest around the time of the perigee. It is advisable to avoid all work involving soil and plants on the day of the perigee itself.

The Moon is closer to the Earth at the perigee; it looks larger at this time and, conversely, smaller at the apogee. In the calendar on pages 54–77, the Moon is shown at its largest near the perigee and at its smallest near the apogee, set in a band that is similarly widest at the perigee and narrowest at the apogee. The point of the perigee is indicated by the letter P and of the apogee by the letter A.

Lunar nodes

The Earth moves in an elliptical orbit, with the Sun as one of its foci. The plane of this ellipse is called the ecliptic. The Moon also moves around an elliptical orbit, with the Earth as a focus. The plane of this ellipse is at an angle of 5° 9' to the ecliptic. As it moves around the Earth, the Moon therefore crosses the ecliptic twice: once when descending – this is the descending node (℧), and once when ascending – which is the ascending node (☊). Experience has shown that disturbances occur when the Moon is at its perigee or its nodes and these are unfavourable times for cultivating the soil, sowing and harvesting.

On the calendar (pages 54–77), the times to be avoided are indicated in red. Obviously, the closer we are to the nodes and the perigee, the more harmful the influence. Since this influence develops gradually, we cannot indicate precisely when it begins and ends; to get an approximate idea of the hours to avoid, however, simply check the time that the red zone begins and ends.

Planetary nodes

The planets also have nodes, just like the Moon. We have taken them into account up to the present in the last band of the calendar on pages 54–77. This year we include them in the note pages (81–111) using the node symbols (℧ ☊) followed by the appropriate planet symbols (☿ ♀ ♂ ♃).

Eclipses

An eclipse takes place when the Moon is new or full, when it is aligned with the Sun and the Earth in the plane of the ecliptic (2): when the Moon is new it is an eclipse of the Sun and when the Moon is full it is an eclipse of the Moon. When the line of the lunar nodes intersects the Earth's

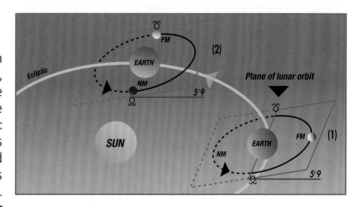

Planes of the EARTH-SUN and MOON-EARTH rotation.

plane of rotation around the Sun and the Moon's plane of rotation around the Earth (1), an eclipse will take place if the node coincides with the New Moon or the Full Moon.

For eclipses in 2008, see the following page.

Eclipses of the Moon in 2008:
- 21 February: total eclipse, reaching its maximum at 03:25 (GMT).
- 16 August: partial eclipse, reaching its maximum at 22:09 (BST).

Eclipses of the Sun in 2008:
- 7 February: annular eclipse reaching its maximum at 03:54 (GMT), visible in New Zealand and the Antarctic.
- 1 August: total eclipse reaching its maximum at 11:21 (BST), visible in Canada, Greenland, Russia, Mongolia, Siberia and China.

The zodiac of the stars

The constellations of the zodiac are groups of stars, named after their various shapes. These constellations are of different sizes. When the Moon passes in front of, or 'through', a constellation, it activates the influences belonging to it and transmits them to us. We owe our understanding of the laws concerning the Moon in the constellations to Rudolf Steiner, the father of anthroposophy. In 1924, he became the founder of biodynamic cultivation and his work has promoted the development of different systems of organic farming.

Centuries ago, the Chaldeans of Mesopotamia imposed a regular structure on the constellations, dividing them into 12 equal parts of 30° in order to mirror the length of their year. These divisions were called signs and the system will be familiar to followers of sun-sign astrology (dates when the sun changes sign and constellation are included, for information only,

on the calendar on pages 54–77). The zodiacal year begins with the sign of Aries in spring, at one of the two points in the year (vernal and autumnal) where the ecliptic crosses the celestial equator (imagine the plane of the terrestrial equator extending into space). In biodynamics (see page 17), the same regular structure is imposed on the lunar cycle. An astronomical phenomenon means that the natural rhythm of the constellations does not correspond exactly with the 'imposed' rhythm of the signs, and because the influences of constellations and signs are different (see below), both are used in biodynamics, sometimes in harmony (see page 12).

The influences of signs and constellations are not the same: the signs affect energy by influencing the fundamental qualities (hot, cold, dry, wet), while the influences of the constellations are more physical and directed towards specific zones, such as plant organs.

The Moon in the zodiac signs

The four fundamental qualities (hot, cold, dry, wet) act upon plants largely through the signs of the zodiac.

Hot tends to assist and accelerate plants' metabolism and helps in the exchange of fluids. Crop production is increased. However, if you actively increase heat, plants could dry out, particularly if there is already internal or external dryness. If there is already too much internal or external moisture, the risk of contracting parasitic or viral diseases increases. 'Hot' helps to counter-balance excessive external 'cold'.

Cold tends to slow down the development of the plant, hinder the exchange of fluids and limit metabolic changes. It also improves resistance to heat.

Dry tends to limit the amount of water in the tissues, concentrates the sap and helps to resist external moisture. Too much can cause the plant to mature too rapidly and wither.

Wet governs the amount of water in plants, which can reach more than 99% of plant mass. It stimulates active principles and nourishes the whole plant. Excess fluid can lead to decomposition and rotting.

- The expansive and vapourizing effects of 'wet' by 'hot' creates **AIR**. Air is therefore hot and wet.
- The condensation of 'wet' by 'cold' creates **WATER**. Water is therefore cold and wet.
- The concentration of 'cold' by 'dry' creates **EARTH**. Earth is therefore cold and dry.

It is not possible, therefore, to apply one quality in isolation. If you want to apply the quality 'dry', you must choose **DRY** and **COLD** (in other words, an **EARTH** sign) or **DRY** and **HOT** (a **FIRE** sign).

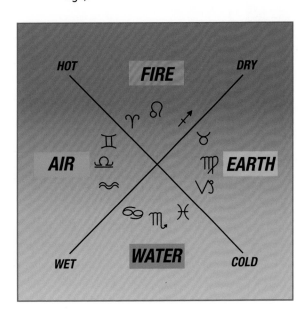

- These qualities cannot exist in isolation; they combine to create the four elements.
- The intensification and concentration of 'hot' by 'dry' creates **FIRE**. Fire is therefore dry and hot.

For example, if you want a specifically dry effect, work alternately when the Moon is in an Earth sign and when it is in a Fire sign; the alternate hot and cold qualities cancel each other out and the dry effect of your work will remain.

The Moon in the constellations

When the Moon is in a **Fire constellation** (Aries, Leo, Sagittarius), plant activity is concentrated mainly in the development of **fruits** and **seeds**. It is a good time for growing tomatoes, French beans, peas, apples and cereals of all kinds (and for maintenance and planting seeds, where appropriate).

When the Moon is in an **Air constellation** (Gemini, Libra, Aquarius), the **flowering** part of a plant grows well, so this is a positive phase for cultivating vegetables such as cauliflowers and artichokes, and ornamental flowers.

When the Moon is in a **Water constellation** (Cancer, Scorpio, Pisces), the **leaf** parts of plants grow well. Now is the time to work on salad vegetables, spinach, chard and so on.

When the Moon is in an **Earth constellation** (Taurus, Virgo, Capricorn), **bark** and **roots** develop well, making it an ideal time to concentrate on carrots, potatoes, asparagus, celery, parsnips and other root vegetables.

When signs and constellations are aligned

Better results are achieved when certain signs and constellations are aligned. We have concentrated on the effects of these alignments on food and wine crops, but further observations will allow us to focus and expand on the effects on other plants.

These alignments are represented in the bands on the calendar (pages 54–77) by letters of the alphabet. For example, 'p' indicates that the sign of Leo coincides with the constellation of Cancer. Varying shades of grey indicate periods corresponding to a letter and the times of changes are noted within the signs and constellations bands.

Planetary aspects

The planets revolve around the Sun at different distances and speeds. Viewed from the Earth, they move constantly across the sky. If we look at two planets at any given moment, they form an angle of which the Earth is the apex. If we see these two planets in alignment, the angle formed with the Earth is 0°. When this happens, they are in conjunction. When one planet sets and the other rises, it is known as an opposition (180°). When the position of a planet creates an angle of 60°, 90° or 120°, it is in aspect. Each aspect has been given its own colour in order to make location easier (see the note pages 81–111).

In the illustration, the Moon is in conjunction with Mercury and the Sun (☽ ☌ ☿ ☉) and also square to Mars (☽ ◻ ♂).

Some of these aspects can promote the harmonization of energy, leading to healthier growth. Others can disrupt the plant's energy, causing such problems as slow growth, excessive growth and disease.

We refer to planetary aspects in several chapters. The days and times when they occur are indicated in the notes pages (81–111).
We have observed that some aspects had a significant influence on a variety of plants over a period of 12 or 24 hours.

Make a note of your own observations and experiences and you will be able to use the knowledge you have acquired in other areas of life, beyond gardening.

Tides

You might think that the influence of the tides is restricted to the movement of water, but in fact tidal influence also affects the soil and most plants. Tides are caused by the gravitational attraction of astronomical bodies; their strength depends on the mass of the bodies and the distance between them. As far as the Earth is concerned, the two bodies with the most significant effect are the Moon and the Sun. The Moon's effect is, on average, 2.17 times stronger than that of the Sun. This attraction subtly alters the shape of the Earth, and this phenomenon is most apparent in the movements of the oceans. As centrifugal force counterbalances the strength of gravitational attraction, the Earth's ocean surface which is naturally shaped like an egg (1), is pulled into the shape of a rugby ball (2).

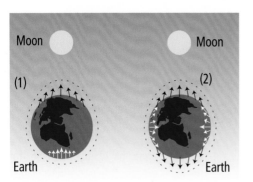

Since the attraction of the Moon is greater, its position determines the tides. The effect of the Sun is limited to reducing or increasing the Moon's gravitational attraction. When the Moon is new or full, the Sun, Moon and Earth are aligned, so the two gravitational pulls combine to cause the highest tides (spring tide). During the first and last quarters, on the other hand, the lunar and solar gravitational attractions oppose one another, so the tides are lower (neap tide).

Atmospheric pressure has a delaying effect on the natural rhythm of the tides, but without this influence the tide would always be at its lowest when the Moon is ascending. During the time the Moon takes to reach its highest point, or meridian (on average 6 hours and 12 minutes), the tide rises (incoming tide) before beginning to recede (ebb tide) until the Moon sets. The tide then rises again to reach the opposite meridian (+180°) before receding once more until the following evening. This double cycle of rising and receding tides takes 24 hours and 50 minutes, the time the Moon takes to return to the same meridian and a little longer than one rotation of the Earth (to compensate for the Moon's displacement during the Earth's rotation).

It is not only the seas that are affected – scientists have shown that the Earth's crust lifts 30 cm (12 in) or more during high tides and it is also known that the tides can affect living creatures. It seems obvious to us that tides have an influence on sap and on crops in general. Although we have not been able to gather together enough evidence to verify the following points, and despite the practical difficulties involved, we consider it useful to take them into account when carrying out certain tasks.

Choose a rising tide for the following:
- sowing, when the Moon is descending to balance energies
- grafting
- cultivating heavy soil
- spreading compost (avoid compacting the compost)
- harvesting, when the Moon is waning

Choose a receding tide for these tasks:
- sowing, when the Moon is ascending to balance energies
- pricking out
- cultivating light soil
- cutting wood
- harvesting, when the Moon is waxing

Tidal influences are not felt immediately, and with plants, the delay is estimated at about an hour. For example, the first effects of a rising tide will be felt about one hour after the Moon rises or sets; the effects will continue until one hour after it reaches the meridian. In the time (up to thirty minutes, in fact) that precedes or follows the change, the effect will be greatly reduced, so avoid these times if you want to get the maximum benefit from your work. The effects of a rising tide are stronger in the morning, while those of a receding tide are stronger in the afternoon. This pattern occurs near the New Moon and the Full Moon; tidal influences are weaker around the 'quarters'.

The times given in the notes pages (81–111) are for GMT standard time (26 October to 29 March) and British Summer Time (30 March to 25 October) – see page 2 for other countries.

The times given for the rising and setting of the Moon are for London. For the times for where you live, see the table, page 2.

On pages 81-111, to make the calculations easier, the time that a rising tide begins to affect plants is marked in green and the time that a receding tide begins to affect plants is marked in black. The times for London are valid for a good part of England. For greater precision, see the time differences marked on the map, right.

TIME DIFFERENCES FROM LONDON

+40   +30   +20   +10   0   -10

For Ireland add 30 minutes to the times indicated. For example, if you want to carry out a crown graft on 26 April and benefit from the effect of the rising tide, do it between 10:00 and 18:45 if you are in the London area. If you are in Ireland, do it between 10:30 and 19:15.

Chinese seasons

The traditional Chinese year is made up of 12 lunar months (13 months in 7 years out of a 19-year cycle), each month beginning at the New Moon and lasting 29 or 30 days. The Chinese New Year takes place between 21 January and 20 February. Chinese springtime is determined by the Sun and begins halfway between the winter solstice and the vernal (spring) equinox. Between each season comes an 'inter-seasonal' period of 18 days that makes it easier to adapt to the change from one season to the next. According to traditional Chinese culture Qi (pronounced chi) is the energy or 'life force' that is present everywhere in the universe and that flows around us as part of that universe. The seasons influence the nature of the Qi. The five elements (wood, fire, earth, metal, water), and all that is linked to them, form the basis of Chinese culture and medicine (see the table below). The main focus of Chinese medicine is on the prevention of illness by taking into account the rhythm and flow of the Qi – treating the patient at the appropriate time enables treatment to work more effectively.

The method used in acupuncture is simple and effective – treatment is given during the inter-seasonal period before the season that governs the part of the body that is affected. For example, for problems involving the element 'water' (such as bladder, kidneys, fatigue and anxiety), treatment is carried out between autumn and winter. By taking into account the patient's Qi, the most effective days for treatment can be selected. As a result, knowledge of the Chinese seasons is extremely useful for practitioners whose work involves energy flow.

ELEMENT	WOOD	FIRE	EARTH	METAL	WATER
SEASON	Spring	Summer	Inter-season	Autumn	Winter
DIRECTION	East	South	Centre	West	North
ORGAN	Liver	Heart	Spleen	Lung	Kidneys
VISCERA	Gall bladder	Small intestine	Stomach	Large intestine	Bladder
TASTE	Acid	Bitter	Sweet	Pungent	Salty
COLOUR	Greeny blue	Red	Yellow	White	Black
ORGAN/SENSE	Eye/sight	Tongue/speech	Mouth/taste	Nose/smell	Ear/hearing
EMOTIONS	Anger	Joy	Thoughtfulness	Sadness	Intense fear
ENERGY	Wind	Heat	Wet	Dry	Cold

Biodynamics

Biodynamics is the study of the dynamic life forces on Earth that have an effect on all living things (plants, trees, animals and humans). They include telluric lines, underground streams and geological fault lines.

For the past fifty years, physicists, doctors and dowsers have demonstrated how a specific location, or soil, can influence the growth or behaviour of plants, trees, animals and people. Dr Hartmann and Dr Curry are both well-known exponents of the theory, having highlighted the existence of electromagnetic fields.

This sickly tree has suffered as a result of being planted on an intersection of electromagnetic lines (causing the double trunk, canker, stunted appearance, smaller leaves and fruit).

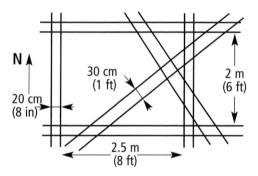

The Hartmann Grid consists of naturally occurring charged lines measuring 20 cm (8 in) in width and occurring at intervals of, on average, 2 m (6 ft) running from north to south and 2.5 m (8 ft) from east to west. The grid is like a large-meshed fishing net covering the Earth, and its influence can be felt even at the top of the highest buildings. The Curry lines measure 30–40 cm (12–16 in) in width and run diagonally to the Hartmann lines and at irregular intervals.

Many animals avoid the lines, including dogs, cattle, horses, pigs, deer, stags and wild boar. Others are drawn to them, such as cats, ants and swallows.

It is advisable not to spend too much time where the lines occur and to take great care over the positioning of furniture and equipment, including beds, workstations and the chair used regularly for watching television. It is important to remember that every living thing positioned directly above the intersection of these lines (the nodes) will be adversely affected at some stage. Pay particular attention to where you plant trees and shrubs and position beehives and animal hutches.

You may already have experienced the effects of electromagnetic fields. If not, it is relatively easy to locate the fields after a few lessons on using a divining rod, a dowsing pendulum, a Hartmann lobe or your own hands.

Hartmann lobe

The Red Moon

This period begins with the New Moon immediately after Easter and ends at the following New Moon. Since Easter is the Sunday following the first Full Moon of spring, **this year the Red Moon lasts from 6 April to 5 May.**

During this time, young shoots and buds can become damaged by the cold even when the air temperature is above zero. This phenomenon is probably due to the balancing of the temperature in the upper atmosphere with the soil temperature, rather than to the light of the Moon. In fact, when the sky is clear, the temperatures are balanced by radiation, which is greater at soil and plant level. As a result, while the temperature in the air may be just above zero, the temperature of the air surrounding plants can fall below zero, scorching young buds and leaves. This balancing occurs throughout the year but only produces this effect during the period of the Red Moon due to the combination of fragile buds and the low soil temperature.

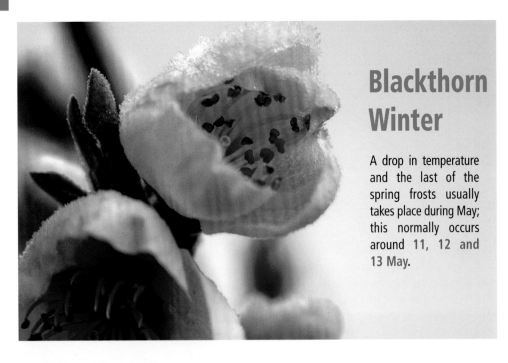

Blackthorn Winter

A drop in temperature and the last of the spring frosts usually takes place during May; this normally occurs around 11, 12 and 13 May.

Indian Summer

Around 11 November, six months after the Blackthorn Winter in May, the exact opposite takes place, and an un-seasonal rise in temperature occurs, known as an Indian Summer.

At both times, it appears as if the previous season is making one last effort to assert itself before the next season takes over.

Crop rotation

Each plant has its own nutritional needs and different plants draw nourishment from different layers of the soil. As a result, growing the same plant in the same place can lead to an imbalance of soil constituents and even the depletion of some, along with an increase in parasites, weeds and diseases. In most instances, it is a good idea to wait for three to five years before growing the same crop in the same place again. You can reduce this period, or even ignore it entirely, for vegetables such as spinach and lettuce, which have a short growth cycle. On the other hand, extend the period for crops such as strawberries and asparagus where the plant itself remains in the same position for several years before being replaced, with an annual harvest of just its fruit. Tomatoes are an exception, as they can be grown in the same position for several years in succession.

There are three key rules of crop rotation:

THE FIRST RULE involves rotating plants according to whether they are grown for their roots, leaves, flowers or fruits. On a single plot of land, grow 'fruit' plants the first year (nitrogen-fixing), then 'flower' plants, then 'leaf' (nitrogen-hungry), and finish with 'root' plants. So, for example, you could plant squash, courgettes, maize and French beans, followed by cauliflowers, broccoli or green manure (phacelia, lupins, clover) which would not be cut until the flowering stage; then cabbages, spinach, lettuces and leeks, and, finally, potatoes, celery, beetroots, onions and carrots. You could achieve several rotations in the same year – for instance, green manure could precede or follow a crop. In addition to the rotation of the different crops, it is also important to bear in mind which plants grow well together (see page 78).

THE SECOND RULE is not to grow two plants of the same botanical family one after the other. The main botanical families are as follows:

- **Chenopodiaceae:** beetroot, spinach, Swiss chard.
- **Compositae:** artichoke, cardoon, chicory, endive, lettuce, dandelion, black salsify, Jerusalem artichoke.
- **Cruciferae:** all types of cabbage, cress, mustard, turnip, radish.
- **Cucurbitaceae:** cucumber, marrow, courgette, melon, pumpkin.
- **Leguminosae:** broad bean, French bean, lentil, alfalfa, pea, clover.
- **Liliaceae:** garlic, asparagus, chive, shallot, onion, leek.
- **Umbelliferae:** carrot, celery, chervil, parsnip, parsley.
- **Solanaceae:** aubergine, capsicum, pepper, potato, tomato.

THE THIRD RULE concerns the amount of manure a crop needs. It is good practice to follow a crop that requires large amounts of manure with one that requires little or none.

- **Crops requiring large amounts of manure:** aubergine, celery, cabbage, spinach, fennel, maize, leek, pepper, potato, tomato.
- **Crops requiring little:** garlic, chervil, cress, shallot, broad bean, French bean, corn salad (lamb's lettuce), onion, radish, lettuce.

Other crops fall between the two extremes, requiring an average amount.

WORKING WITH THE MOON

WATERING: to avoid plants developing shallow roots, instead of watering little and often, water them generously but less frequently. The ideal time is when the Moon is in the descendant and in the constellation of Virgo, Gemini or Libra. Avoid nodes and the superposition of the sign of Leo with the constellation of Leo.

MULCHING: mulch helps to fertilize and protect the soil, and limits the evaporation of moisture and weed germination.

A variety of materials can be used as mulch, such as straw, grass cuttings (a thin layer, fresh or dried), composted bark (very effective, a thickness of 2 or 3 cm/about 1 inch is enough).

It is best to mulch when the Moon is waxing and in an Earth or Air sign.

Aeration of the soil should ideally be carried out when the Moon is ascending; soil decomposes and breaks down more easily (via worms and micro-organisms) when the Moon is descending.

STRAWBERRIES: separate and plant out runners during the constellation of Leo ♌ preferably when the sign of Leo ♌ is in superposition with the constellation of Leo ♌ (g) for example, from 18:00 on 25 September until 14:53 on 26 September.

> Each time we cultivate the soil, we can modify or increase any influences. If you have sown a crop at an unfavourable time, you can reverse the effect to a certain degree by hoeing at a favourable time.

SOWING: always choose a constellation appropriate to the crop you are sowing (ie. favourable to fruit, root, flower or leaf plants) and preferably sow in the morning. If possible choose one with the maximum number of stars indicated in the lowest band (summarising lunar and planetary influences) on the calendar on pages 54–77.

PLANTING AND PRICKING OUT: choose days when the Moon is descending and also, if possible, when it is opposite a constellation appropriate to the crop that you are growing (ie. favourable to fruit, root, flower or leaf plants) and preferably in the afternoon.

HOEING: for eradicating weeds see page 29.
IN WET WEATHER: if possible, weed in the morning in a Fire or Air sign when the Moon is waning.
IN DRY WEATHER: weed in the evening, if possible, and in an Earth or Water sign when the Moon is waxing.

> **THE END PRODUCT:** always bear in mind the kind of crop you are growing. Take endives as an example – sow and hoe them on dates favourable to 'root' plants in order to help the roots develop well, but, to ensure a good crop, harvest them on dates favourable to 'leaf' plants when the Moon is descending. Their growth should be forced on a good 'leaf' date when the Moon is ascending.

GREEN SALAD: until July, sow green salad in a Water constellation when the Moon is waning in order to prevent these plants from going to seed. During the autumn many forms of energy are in decline. To compensate, sow green salad in a Water constellation, but when the Moon is waxing.

POTATOES: plant potatoes on a day favourable to 'root' plants, but not too close to the perigee. To raise seed potatoes, plant when the Moon is in the sign of Taurus.

To avoid producing green potatoes, earth up when the Moon is in an Earth constellation and when it is waning and also, if possible, with a receding tide.

To remove the eyes (buds) from potatoes that have been lifted and stored so that they will keep longer, choose a time when the Moon is waning and descending, and prefer-ably when it is in the constellation of Virgo.

CROP ROTATION: see page 19.

Pleasing to the eye and beneficial for the plants, grown in the right combinations, plants can work well together (see pages 78–9).

Daily rhythms

The Earth's energy patterns vary according to the seasons. During spring, when the Sun is ascend-ing, the Earth 'breathes out', whereas in the autumn, the Sun descends and the Earth 'breathes in'. The same pattern is echoed by the Moon when it is ascending (sometimes called the lunar spring) and when it is descending (also known as the lunar autumn). And energies rise and fall through-out the day too, rising in the morning when the Earth 'breathes out' – a good time to sow (for example, carrots during the morning of a day favourable to 'root' plants), to weed in wet weather, and to harvest aerial plant parts. In the afternoon, the Earth 'breathes in' so it is a good time to plant, prick out, plough, weed in dry weather and harvest root crops. The inter-vening period, from 12:00 to 15:00, is a period of transition and is best avoided.

Horticulture

BULBS: plant bulbs when the Moon is in the constellation of Libra (♎).

REPOTTING: repot plants when the Moon is descending.
- Choose a date favourable to 'leaf' plants for those grown for their foliage (♋ or ♏).
- For flowering plants, choose a date favourable to 'flower' plants (♊ or ♎).

FERTILIZING: add fertilizer when the Moon is descending and if possible, when it is waxing, avoiding Fire signs.

GRAFTING ROSES: shield budding can be carried out during any month of the year on a date favourable to 'flower' plants when the Moon is ascending. Graft as low down the stem as possible towards the base to prevent suckers from forming.

PRUNING ROSES: choose a 'flower' date when the Moon is descending. All roses should be pruned when they are dormant or semi-dormant, ie. between autumn and when the buds are just beginning to break out in the spring, but avoiding frosty periods. Prune to an outward facing bud, removing dead, diseased and dying shoots and any crossing growth. Pruning will also help to prevent damage to tall stems caused by wind rock. Most modern roses flower on new or the current season's growth and so should normally be pruned fairly hard to stimulate new growth and to encourage flowering. Shrub and old garden roses should be pruned lightly.

- **Cluster-flowering bush roses (Floribunda):** cut back main stems to 30–40 cm (12–16 in) from the ground or, for taller cultivars, to about one third of their length.
- **Large-flowering bush roses (Hybrid Tea):** cut back to 20–25 cm (8–10 in) from the ground, or slightly less severely in very mild areas.
- **Climbing and rambling roses:** climbers should not normally be pruned in their first two years except to remove dead or diseased stems. In subsequent years shorten side shoots and leave main shoots unpruned unless they are too long. Shorten the side shoots of ramblers in the first two years to a vigorous shoot. In subsequent years cut back old or diseased stems to ground level to maintain a good framework and allow air to circulate freely.
- **Shrub and old garden roses:** prune only lightly – these flower on wood that is two or more years old.

PRUNING FLOWERING SHRUBS: remove dead or diseased stems and any suckers at the base of the plant, retaining the strongest stems. Prune above a lateral bud on a date favourable to 'flower' plants with a descending Moon.

- **flowering shrubs (old wood):** prune as soon as flowering is over (eg. forsythia).
- **flowering shrubs (new wood):** prune quite hard when the worst of the cold weather is over at the beginning of spring (eg. buddleia).

Cultivating trees and shrubs

PLANTING

The following rules are important for planting a tree:

Location: avoid very windy positions, and see Biodynamics (page 17).

Soil: ensure it is well balanced – for instance, if it is too acidic, add lime-rich material such as mushroom compost, but if is too heavy, dig in some sand.

Time of year: avoid heavy frosts. Plant trees in the autumn preferably, provided that the following winter is not likely to be too hard. You can also plant in spring but you will need to water young trees more regularly during the following summer. Whatever season they are planted in, trees need a lot of attention during the first few years before they become established (watering, aerating the soil, adding compost).

Planting: it is essential to avoid the lunar nodes (in the case of an eclipse, wait for two days) as well as times when the Moon is square to the Sun, Mars or Saturn (☾ ▢ ☉ ♂ ♄) – see pages 81–111.

- **Flowering and fruit-bearing trees and bushes:** plant when the Moon is descending, if possible when it is also waxing and when the tide is receding. If the Moon is waning, choose a time that corresponds with a rising tide.
- **Deciduous trees and shrubs:** mainly as for flowering and fruit-bearing trees above, except for trees that grow quickly and those that tend to 'rush' (poplars, maples), when it is better to plant with the Moon ascending and waning and with a receding tide. This configuration produces softer wood but it will encourage this type of tree to grow more quickly and with fewer knots.
- **Conifers:** plant when the Moon is in the descendant and if possible waning. This helps conifers such as firs to develop deeper roots.

PRUNING

As a general rule, prune when the Moon is descending, although an exception can be made when pruning a young tree since the ascending Moon will encourage new wood to grow more quickly. Avoid lunar nodes, when the Moon is square to the Sun, Mars or Saturn (☾ ▢ ☉ ♂ ♄) – see pages 81–111 – as well as the perigee, the equinox and periods of severe cold.

- **Fruit trees and bushes:** prune when the Moon is descending, and if possible when it is also waning and when there is a rising tide.

- **Flowering shrubs:** prune when the Moon is descending, and if possible when it is also waxing and when there is a receding tide.

- **Conifers, deciduous trees and hedges:** prune when the Moon is descending, if possible when it is waxing and with a rising tide. However, prune cypress trees, pyracanthas and trees and hedges that have reached their desired height when the Moon is waning rather than waxing.

GRAFTING

Choose an ascending Moon, on a date favourable to 'fruit' plants preferably or on a date favourable to 'flower' plants if this is not possible. Remove and heel in the grafts when the Moon is ascending (in December/January in the UK).

- **Crown graft:** this form of graft is preferable to cleft grafting, which often causes canker and fruit scab. Wait until the rootstock begins to flower so that there is plenty of sap rising and graft on a date favourable to 'fruit' plants when the Moon is ascending, for example 26 April.

- **Shield budding:** this should be carried out in August on a 'fruit' day with a rising moon when the sap is rising for the second time, for example 22 August. To ensure plenty of rising sap, water the rootstock during the fortnight before the grafting. Make the 'shield' from the thin bark of the rootstock, with just a little of the wood attached – by leaving a strip of wood, you prevent the grafted bud from falling out.

PROPAGATING WITH CUTTINGS

Ideally, cuttings should be taken just as the Moon is coming to the end of its ascension and should be planted as it begins to descend.

- **Cuttings from bushes:** (such as gooseberries, blackcurrants, etc.) in autumn, on the last day of the ascending Moon, take cuttings of around 10–15 cm (4–6 in) in length from the current year's growth. Gather the cuttings together in bunches of ten or so, and gently hold the stems together with a rubber band, place them in a plastic bag and leave them for a day in the refrigerator. When the Moon begins its descent, plant the cuttings out at an angle of about 45°, leaving a little less than half the cutting above ground. Planting at this angle helps promote their growth. In spring, as soon as the first leaves appear and when the Moon is descending, gently lift the cuttings and place each in a pot full of enriched peat. A few weeks later, when the roots have developed, plant them out or pot them on in soil-based compost. Propagating cuttings in bunches has been seen to increase hormonal activity, resulting in improved growth.

Harvesting

Various factors influence the quality and preservation of fruit and vegetables after harvest. As a general rule, choose an ascending Moon for harvesting plant parts that grow above ground and a descending Moon for parts that grow below ground, but avoid the perigee, lunar nodes and stormy weather. Fruit and vegetables that do not store well will last much longer if you avoid harvesting during Water signs and constellations (Cancer, Scorpio and Pisces). On the harvesting band on the calendar on pages 54–77, look for the days marked with stars – green stars for aerial parts and yellow for roots.

Other factors to take into account:

- Fruit picked when the Moon is ascending will stay juicy for longer and will have more energy-giving properties.
- The ascending Moon will also help plants to develop and ripen.
- The descending Moon promotes the preservation of certain properties in harvested crops.

As there are many different factors that need to be taken into account we have produced a quick-reference summary:

- Harvest fruit that should be allowed to ripen as slowly as possible (strawberries, raspberries, cherries, apricots, peaches, plums, etc.) when the Moon is waxing and descending (if need be, when it is ascending and waning) and if possible on days with one of the following planetary aspects (☾ ☌ ⚹ △ ♀ - ☾ ☌ ☿ - ☾ ☌ ⚼ ☍) see pages 81–111.

- For squashes and varieties of pumpkin that do not keep well, choose a waxing (but not ascending) Moon during the following periods: *a - b - i - j - k - L - q - r - s - t - z -* (see the calendar on pages 54–77) and if possible pick them during one of the following aspects (☾ ☌ ⚹ △ ♀ - ☾ △ ☉) see pages 81–111. For example, AUGUST: 2* - 3 - 4 - 5 - 6 - 7 am* - 12 pm - 13* - 14 - 31 - SEPTEMBER: 1* - 2 - 3 - 9 - 10* - 29 pm - 30 (am = morning, pm = afternoon).

- When harvesting root crops, follow the guidelines on the calendar (pages 54–77) and try to combine the descending with the waning Moon, except in the case of garlic, onions and shallots, when you should choose the waxing Moon.

We believe that the tides also affect the harvest (see page 14). When the Moon is waxing choose a receding tide and when it is waning choose a rising tide. The best time to harvest crops is when these periods occur in the early morning with dew on the ground, as this gives positive and magnetic energy to the harvested crops.

Compost

Composting is the process by which animal or plant waste decomposes and breaks down into a substance that is both nourishing and easily assimilated by the soil's micro-organisms. A combination of plant waste and animal manure is normally required in order to ensure the constituents of the compost are in the correct proportions.

The composting process can normally be activated by adding stinging nettles (with their seeds heads removed) and comfrey, either as plants or in the form of a liquid. Good compost should be well oxygenated and loosely packed, not compacted. When it is ready to use, it should be light, rich and have a pleasant smell of humus, so it is important to make it at just the right moment. We have summarised all the different factors that will help you to produce good compost in the table below, including certain Moon/Pluto aspects.

COMPOST

	1	2	3	4	5	6	7	8	9	10	11	12	13	14	15	16	17	18	19	20	21	22	23	24	25	26	27	28	29	30	31
JANUARY										★	★		★					★	★	★									★★		
FEBRUARY						★	★	★	★					★	★	★									★						
MARCH				★								★	★	★									★								
APRIL									★	★	★							★	★★											★★	
MAY						★	★	★									★★	★★								★					
JUNE			★											★							★										
JULY											★★																★				
AUGUST						★★									★			★	★												
SEPTEMBER		★★		★			★						★	★	★★																★
OCTOBER	★							★	★			★	★	★	★				★							★★	★★				
NOVEMBER						★		★	★★														★★	★★							
DECEMBER		★		★★	★	★								★	★							★★							★		★
	1	2	3	4	5	6	7	8	9	10	11	12	13	14	15	16	17	18	19	20	21	22	23	24	25	26	27	28	29	30	31

(★) the more stars, the more favourable the day

▮ a good time to add to or turn compost heaps that generate a high internal temperature (the majority of compost heaps)

▯ choose these dates for working on slower acting compost heaps that generate less heat (often preferred by farmers and gardeners who practise biodynamics)

▮ recommended for surface composting with non-rotted manure (broken down by worms);

▮ a vertical line dividing a date box indicates morning (left) or afternoon (right)

▬ a date box divided by a horizontal line indicates it is favourable for a certain type of composting (green for high temperature compost and orange for surface composting)

MANURE: spread manure when the Moon is descending, if possible on days marked orange (see the table above).

Fungicides and insecticides

We recommend the use of natural products, both for the sake of the environment and to produce a better quality of crop. You can also use liquid fertilizers to prevent cryptogamic diseases such as those caused by fungi (see below and page 28).

A **decoction of horsetail** is very good for controlling fungal disease. Use about 50 g (2 oz) of horsetail per litre of water (1½ pints) and boil it for 20 minutes. Then dilute with water in the proportion of 1:5 and spray on the leaves or directly on the soil, several times between spring and autumn. If you use sulphur or Bordeaux mixture it is also possible to add horsetail decoction, or liquid fertilizer made from stinging nettles or compost in order to increase the efficiency and reduce the dosage.

Insecticides: a decoction of comfrey can be used to treat tomato whitefly (see page 28) and a decoction of many other plants can be used to produce natural insecticides, such as wormwood, pyrethrum, English ivy, etc. The table below indicates those dates that are the most favourable for applying insecticides and fungicides. The greater the number of stars (★) the more effective will be the application.

☐ favourable for insecticides
■ favourable for fungicides

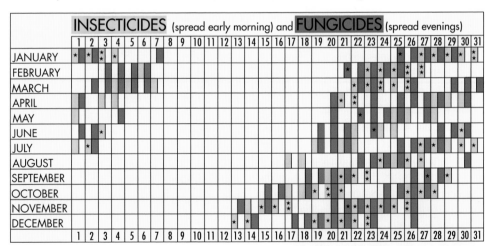

INSECTICIDES (spread early morning) and **FUNGICIDES** (spread evenings)

	1	2	3	4	5	6	7	8	9	10	11	12	13	14	15	16	17	18	19	20	21	22	23	24	25	26	27	28	29	30	31
JANUARY
FEBRUARY
MARCH
APRIL
MAY
JUNE
JULY
AUGUST
SEPTEMBER
OCTOBER
NOVEMBER
DECEMBER

Plant-based decoctions

A plant-based decoction used as a liquid fertilizer provides a natural way of feeding plants and preventing certain diseases. Those made from stinging nettle or comfrey are best known, but other plants can be used such as horsetail, camomile, marigold, achillea or dandelion, either individually or in combination.

Stinging nettles

Whichever plant you choose, the process for **making liquid fertilizer** remains the same. Cut up the fresh plants into small pieces and soak them in water (use 1 kg/2 lb of plants per 10 litres/15 pints of water) and leave it to steep for between one and four weeks – use a wooden or stoneware container, or even plastic if necessary, never use a metal container. Stir the liquid from time to time to help it ferment; then filter out the plant pulp. Use the resulting liquid fertilizer diluted in the proportion of 1:10–20, as appropriate.

WHEN TO MAKE A PLANT DECOCTION

- **To protect against fungal disease:** begin making the decoction when the Moon is waxing and, if possible, when it is also descending. The Moon in conjunction, sextile and trine with the Sun (☾ ☌ ✳ △ ☉) as well as superposition (q), will improve its effectiveness even more.
  Favourable dates are: MARCH: 16 pm - 18 pm - APRIL: 10 pm - 14 after 18:00 - MAY: 9 pm - 14 pm - JUNE: 13 - JULY: 3 - 6 am - 7 pm - 12 pm - AUGUST: 1 pm - 2 pm - 6 am - 11 pm - SEPTEMBER: 4 pm - 29 - OCTOBER: 4 pm - 29. If you also take into account the influence of the rising tide on these dates (see p14), the result will be even better (am = morning, pm = afternoon).

- **To use as a plant feed:** begin making the decoction when the Moon is waxing, and if possible when it is also ascending. The Moon in conjunction, sextile and trine with the Sun (☾ ☌ ✳ △ ☉) will strengthen its influence.

Very favourable dates are: MARCH: 12 am - APRIL: 6 - 10 - MAY: 5 pm - JUNE: 4 am - SEPTEMBER: 10 - OCTOBER: 9 pm (am = morning, pm = afternoon). Make the most of the receding tide on these dates to improve the result even more. Liquid fertilizer made from plants should preferably be used when the Moon is descending and, if possible, when it is also on the wane.

DECOCTION OF STINGING NETTLE

- To use as a fertilizer follow the instructions top left, leave the nettles to steep in water for three weeks and then dilute in the proportion of 1:10 if it is to be spread on the soil, but in at least 1:20 if it is to be sprayed on leaves.
- To prevent fungal diseases, let the mixture steep for a week and then dilute it in the proportion of 1:15–20. The fresh plant can also be used – for example, when potting up tomatoes, put a handful of nettles in the planting hole.

DECOCTION OF COMFREY

A decoction made from comfrey helps combat tomato whitefly, but comfrey really comes into its own as a fertilizer. Fresh leaves can be laid on the soil surface, wilted leaves can be dug into the soil, or it can be used in a liquid fertilizer. To make the liquid feed, soak the leaves in water (see top left this page) for two to four weeks and then dilute in the proportion of 1:10 if applying it directly to the soil or 1:20 if spraying it on leaves.

LIQUID FERTILIZER MADE FROM COMPOST

This is made by mixing one part well-rotted compost to ten parts water and leaving it to steep for one to two weeks. It is effective against cryptogamic (fungal) diseases when sprayed on the leaves of a plant and works on two fronts: it reinforces the plant's immune defences as well as destroying certain fungal spores.

Comfrey

Agriculture

ERADICATING WEEDS

Dig over the soil when the Moon is in the constellation of Leo, which favours germination (marked in green ■ in the following table). This will encourage the majority of any weed seeds present in the soil to germinate. The seedlings of annual weeds can then be dug back into the soil (but perennial weed seedlings are best dug out). This will be most effective in the middle of the day, on the days immediately after the Full Moon. The best way to prevent weeds from germinating is to dig over the soil and sow on moonless nights (along with moisture it is light and warmth that activate seed germination). You can also restrict weed germination by working the soil on the dates marked in yellow ☐.

- **Thistles:** remove thistles when the soil is dry to help prevent them from seeding too easily. They are difficult to eradicate, but for the best results, work in the middle of the day on the dates marked in purple ■ or blue ☐ on the chart below. These dates are also the best for dealing with convolvulus.

CULTIVATING THE SOIL: the work of ploughing, planting, pricking out and spreading compost or manure is best carried out when the Moon is descending. If possible, combine the descending Moon with the waxing Moon when working on light, sandy soil, especially when the weather is dry. In the case of heavy clay soil, if possible, combine the descending Moon with the waning Moon, particularly during wet weather.

- **Dock weed:** dig up dock weed on dates marked in purple ■ or orange ☐.

Choose dates marked with stars (★).
If you have no option other than to dig the soil on dates when there are nodes, dig it over again a few days later to help reinstate positive influences.

If only a part of the day is favourable, the time is indicated by a vertical line (the left section for the morning, the right for the afternoon – see above and left for the key to the colours) ☐. On days that are divided horizontally, two favourable aspects are recommended, as indicated by the two colours ▦. For example, the morning of 9 January after 09:00 is favourable for restricting germination and the afternoon for pulling up thistles.

CLEARING LAND: to clear land of plants such as thorns and brambles, dig them up or cut them down at the perigee and if possible when the waning Moon is close to becoming new (for instance: MAY: 5 - 6 am - JUNE: 3** - JULY: 1 pm - 2 am) (am = morning, pm = afternoon).

MANURE: manure is absorbed by the soil more effectively when the Moon is descending and, if possible, waxing, but avoid spreading manure during Fire signs.

- Seaweed and natural phosphates (such as in bone meal): see 'Manure' left.
- Leaf mould (minerals): spread leaf compost in the morning (but in the evening if the forecast is dry and hot), with an ascending and if possible a waning Moon. Avoid Fire signs.
- Chicken manure: to avoid burning meadow grass, spread chicken manure when the Moon is ascending and, if possible, waxing. Water and Air signs are also preferable.
- Cattle slurry: spread cattle slurry when the Moon is waning and avoid Fire signs.

Hay

A permanent wild flower meadow

- Quality: hay will be of better quality if it is cut when the Moon is ascending and if possible also waning. The aspects Moon sextile or trine Sun (☽ ✳ △ ☉) will improve the quality still further.

For example, the following dates will be favourable: APRIL: 25 pm* - 26* - 27* - 28 am* - 29 am* - 30* - MAY: 1 am* - 1 pm* - 2 pm - 3 - 4 pm* - 5 am* - 22 am* - 23* - 24* - 25** - 26* - 27* - 28 after 8:00 - 30* - 31 - JUNE: 1* - 2* - 19* - 20* - 21* - 22 before 18:00* - 23 after 07:00* - 24 am** - 24 pm* - 25 am* - 27 - 28 am - 28 pm** - 29* - JULY: 1 before 18:00* - 18 after 10 am* - 19* - 21* - 22 before 18:00* - 23 pm* - 24 - 25 before 15:00 - 26* - 27* - 28* (am = morning, pm = afternoon).

When cutting hay, always avoid times that are close to lunar nodes, the perigee (including about 6 hours before and after) and the following aspects: Moon square Sun, Mars and Saturn (☽ ☐ ☉ ♂ ♄) (about 4 hours before and 2 hours after).

- Regrowth: to promote rapid regrowth, cut hay when the waxing Moon is associated with an ascending Moon.

For example: MAY: 5 pm** - 6 after 10:00* - 7* - JUNE: 4 am* - JULY: 16* - 17* (am = morning, pm = afternoon).

Cereal crops

Sow cereal crops on a day favourable to 'fruit' plants, but if this is not possible, choose days favourable to 'flower' and if not 'root' plants. Days favourable to 'leaf' plants are the least beneficial. Also take the following information into consideration to improve results even further. It is organized according to the type of cereal crop.

OATS, WHEAT, BARLEY, RYE

- **Sow:** preferably when the Moon is ascending and if possible waning, with a receding tide.
- **Harvest:** on days favourable to 'root' or 'flower' plants with the Moon waxing and ascending (on dates favourable to 'fruit' plants there is more dust in the air and the risk of weevils is greater, on 'leaf' dates there is a greater risk of fermentation).

    Examples of favourable dates are: JUNE: 21 - 22 - 23 - 24 - 25 am - 30 - JULY: 18 pm - 19 - 20 pm - 21 - 22 before 18:00 - 27 - 28 - AUGUST: 17 - 18 - 23 pm - 24 - 25 am (am = morning, pm = afternoon). Combine the influence of a rising tide with these dates.

The waxing and descending Moon can be suitable mainly when the soil is heavy.

MILLET

- **Sow:** when the Moon is ascending and if possible waxing.
- **Harvest:** when the Moon is waxing and if possible ascending, but avoid 'leaf' dates.

MAIZE, SUNFLOWERS

- **Sow:** preferably when the Moon is ascending and if possible waning, with a rising tide.
- **Harvest:** when the Moon is ascending, avoiding dates favourable to 'leaf' plants.

OILSEED RAPE

- **Sow:** preferably when the Moon is ascending and if possible also waning.
- **Harvest:** when the Moon is waning and ascending, avoiding 'leaf' dates.

Animal husbandry

COVERING: for cows and mares, the best time is between the first quarter and the Full Moon in Fire and Earth signs and, if possible, with the Moon in the descendent. For ewes, the period between the first quarter and the Full Moon during Earth and Air signs is best, with an ascendant Moon if possible. Avoid the perigee and the lunar nodes if possible.

TRIMMING THE FEET OF LIVESTOCK: carry out this task in the signs of Taurus, Leo, Virgo, Sagittarius or Capricorn when the weather is calm or wet and, if possible, when the Moon is waxing. Avoid stormy or icy periods.

SHOEING: choose the waning Moon, particularly when it is in Earth or Air signs.

WORMING: this should be done two or three days before the New Moon or, if this proves impossible, two or three days before the Full Moon.

CLEANING & DISINFECTING COWSHEDS: this will be most effective when the Moon is waxing and in a Fire or Earth sign.

MATING RABBITS: results will be best between the New Moon and the first quarter.

MALE OR FEMALE CHICKS: eggs collected around the time of the last quarter will produce mainly male chicks. For female chicks, eggs should be collected around the first quarter. For best results, incubate the eggs so that they hatch between the New Moon and the first quarter.

WHEN TO START OUTDOOR GRAZING: choose the following correlations of signs and constellations: a - b - c* - d* - k* - L* - m - n - s* - t* - x (see page 12). For example, MARCH: 2 - 3 - 4* - 5* - 13* - 14* - 15 - 16 - 22* - 23* - 27 - 28 - 29 - 30 - 31 - APRIL: 1* - 2 am* - 9* - 10* - 11 - 12 - 17 pm* - 18* - 19* - 23 - 24 - 25 pm - 26 - 27 - 28* - 29 am* - MAY: 7* - 8 - 9 - 15* - 16* - 17* - 20 pm - 21 - 23 - 24 - 25* - 26* (am = morning, pm = afternoon).

MOVING CATTLE: move cattle between the day after the first quarter and the day before the last quarter, to reduce damage to grass.

BRINGING CATTLE IN: cowsheds will be dryer in winter if cattle are brought inside during autumn when the Moon is passing through the constellation of Leo.

TO AVOID: In addition to the above, avoid turning out, moving or bringing in animals on the following days: JANUARY: 11 pm - 12 am - 19 am - 22 - 24 - FEBRUARY: 1 - 8 - 20 pm - 21 - 28 pm - MARCH: 6 - 19 - 21 - APRIL: 2 pm - 15 - 20 - 29 pm - 30 am - MAY: 6 - 12 - 20 am - JUNE: 3 pm - 9 am - 18 - 30 pm - JULY: 5 pm - 14 am - 18 - 20 am - 21 pm - AUGUST: 3 - 16 - 24 pm - 26 am - 29 - SEPTEMBER: 7 - 12 pm - 14 pm - 15 - 20 am - 27pm - OCTOBER: 7 am - 12 am - 14 - 17 am - 18 pm - 22 pm - NOVEMBER: 1 - 6 am - 13 - 14 am - 18 pm - 21 pm - DECEMBER: 6 - 12 - 19 am - 26 am - 30 am (am = morning, pm = afternoon).

Beekeeping

BEES

For the best results, work with bees during the following constellations.

During Fire constellations to benefit the queens and increase the production of honey.

During Air constellations to benefit the queens and to encourage the development of young bees.

During Earth constellations to maximise the cell-building instinct. Honey collected during Earth constellations will set more quickly.

Avoid all work with bees during Water constellations – these periods have an adverse effect on the hives and honey.

Extract honey in a Fire or Air constellation.

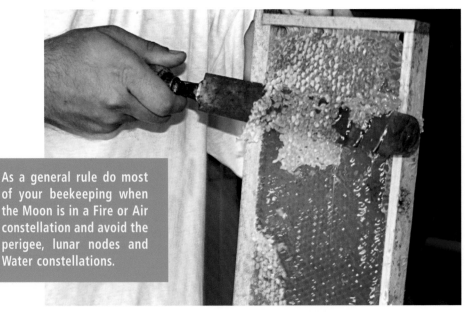

As a general rule do most of your beekeeping when the Moon is in a Fire or Air constellation and avoid the perigee, lunar nodes and Water constellations.

Winegrowing

PRUNING GRAPE VINES

Prune grape vines when the Moon is both descending and, if possible, waxing, with a rising tide. Avoid the lunar nodes and when the Moon is squared with Saturn (☾ ◻ ♄).

DISBUDDING

Disbud when the Moon is waning and, if possible, descending, with a receding tide. Disbudding with the Moon sextile or trine Sun or Mars (☾ ✳ △ ☉ ♂) should reduce the growth of suckers (see pages 81–111).

POLLARDING AND CUTTING BACK

Carry out this work when the Moon is descending, with a receding tide and, if possible, with one of the planetary aspects mentioned above.

HARVESTING GRAPES

An ascending Moon will give a better yield but the wine produced will keep better when the Moon is descending. To improve the quality of the wine and reinforce its character, harvest the grapes according to the constellations. Choose dates favourable to 'fruit' plants for fruity wines, 'root' days for vines grown where the soil plays an important part in the flavour, and 'flower' days for more floral wines. Avoid lunar nodes: they can hinder the development of aromas.

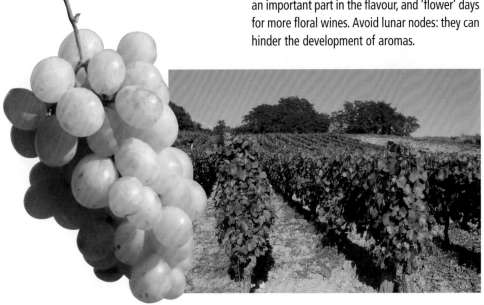

Cider making

DECANT

Decant cider when the Moon is waxing and descending if possible, and with a rising tide. Choose days when the weather is calm, preferably early in the morning with dew on the ground.

BOTTLE

Bottle cider when the Moon is waning and descending, preferably in the constellations of Virgo (♍) or Leo (♌) and, if possible, with a rising tide. Avoid days when the Moon is squared with Mars, Jupiter, Saturn or the Sun (☾ ◻ ♂ ♃ ♄ ☉) – see pages 81–111. Also avoid stormy, windy and very cold weather.

Beer making

WHEN TO START

Make your beer when the Moon is descending and, if possible, waxing, with a rising tide. Moon–Venus aspects (☾ ☍ ♂ △ ✳ ♀), except square, are very favourable. Avoid lunar nodes, the perigee and dates when the Moon is squared with Mars, Jupiter, Saturn or the Sun (☾ ◻ ♂ ♃ ♄ ☉) – see pages 81–111. For the best results use hops picked when the Moon is ascending and with the influence of a rising tide.

BOTTLE

Bottle beer when the Moon is descending and, if possible, between the last and first quarters. Choose a time influenced by a rising tide to help with the development of aromas. Choose an Air sign if possible, and avoid stormy, windy and very cold weather.

Forestry

If possible, only cut down trees after they have lost their leaves, but while the Sun is still in the descendent (before the winter solstice).

TIMBER

Cut timber when the Moon is descending but avoid the last day of this phase. The wood will react differently according to the sign of the zodiac that the Moon is in.

The day on which wood is both cut and used is very important.

- To avoid **parasites** and **rotting**, cut wood in the following signs: Leo ■, Virgo ■, Scorpio ■ or Sagittarius ■.
- To prevent wood from **warping and splintering**, cut it during Libra ■ or, better still, in Scorpio ■.
- Cut wood to be used for **frameworks for buildings and other structures** in Leo ■, Virgo ■, Libra ■, Scorpio ■ or Sagittarius ■.
- Wood for **tools** should be cut in Leo ■, Virgo ■ or Libra ■.
- To prevent the softwood from coniferous trees from **flaking**, cut it in Scorpio ■ or Sagittarius ■.
- **The superposition of the sign and constellation of Leo (q) is a good time for cutting wood,** for example from 05:00 on 19 November to 01:14 on 20 November.
- When the sap is flowing, leave a felled tree for several weeks before removing the branches (the leaves draw out the sap).

Useful tip: to prevent wood from warping when you are using it (for frames, cladding, etc.), choose these dates [____], especially those marked with stars (★).

In the table below, the signs are represented by colours for easier reference:

Cancer: ■ Leo: ■ Virgo: ■ Libra: ■ Scorpio: ■ Sagittarius: ■

Those planetary aspects that will improve the wood are shown by a star. Those that are harmful are coloured in red ■.

WOOD

	1	2	3	4	5	6	7	8	9	10	11	12	13	14	15	16	17	18	19	20	21	22	23	24	25	26	27	28	29	30	31
JANUARY	★	★		★	★		★					★	★															★	★	★	
FEBRUARY		★				★		★	★			★	★					★	★				★					★			
MARCH					★			★				★	★				★	★				★	★	★							
APRIL			★					★	★									★	★		★								★		
MAY	★			★		★	★				★				★		★		★		★							★			
JUNE		★										★																★			
JULY	★			★	★		★		★			★														★				★	
AUGUST		★					★			★												★					★		★		
SEPTEMBER	★			★			★																	★	★				★		
OCTOBER																			★	★	★				★	★		★	★		
NOVEMBER				★	★														★		★								★	★	
DECEMBER			★	★												★	★			★		★							★	★	
	1	2	3	4	5	6	7	8	9	10	11	12	13	14	15	16	17	18	19	20	21	22	23	24	25	26	27	28	29	30	31

FIREWOOD: cut firewood when the Moon is descending, avoiding days close to the New Moon. Stack firewood when the Moon is descending, if possible between the first and last quarter – it will dry better then.

CHRISTMAS TREES: cut Christmas trees when the Moon is ascending and waxing to stop them shedding their needles too quickly. The following aspects will strengthen this effect – Moon sextile, trine or square Sun or Venus (☾ ✳ △ ▢ ☉ ♀) – see pages 108–111.

Miscellaneous

WORKING ON BOATS ON DRY LAND: carry out painting work when the Moon is in the descendant during periods (a, b, c, i, j, k). The following aspects can be beneficial: Moon sextile or trine Sun (☾ ✳ △ ☉) and Moon conjunction Jupiter (☾ ☌ ♃). Avoid the nodes and Moon square Sun (☾ ▢ ☉). Return boats to the water when the Moon is waning, if possible between the last quarter and the New Moon and when the Moon is in an Earth or Air sign.

CHIMNEYS: to improve the 'draw' of a chimney in autumn, light the fire during an ascending Moon, on a day favourable to 'fruit' and, if possible, between the Full Moon and the final quarter. Sweep chimneys when the Moon is in the constellation of Pisces between the New Moon and the first quarter.

MOSS ON TILES, SALT DEPOSITS ON BRICKWORK, MOULD: remove when the Moon is waxing and ascending, avoiding Water signs and constellations. The nodes, the perigee and the Moon squared with the Sun and Saturn (☾ ▢ ☉ ♄) are all favourable, and a drying wind will help.

DRAIN SOIL: when the Moon is ascending.

PATHS AND COURTYARDS: to work on paths and courtyards, choose (the best are marked *): FEBRUARY: 20 am - 20 pm - MARCH: 18 pm* - 19 am* - APRIL: 15 am** - 15 pm* - MAY: 12** - JUNE: 8** - JULY: 5 pm* - 6 am* - AUGUST: 2* (am = morning, pm – afternoon).

TRENCHES: the sides of trenches dug or cleaned out when the Moon is ascending may erode more quickly, especially if the soil is light, but should not fall in completely. Trenches dug when the Moon is descending tend to erode and collapse. Choose a time close to the Full Moon to help trenches last longer.

SPRINGS: begin work to collect spring water on the day of the New Moon and when the Moon is ascending (water is lost when it is descending).

MUSHROOMS: usually emerge a few days after the New Moon and are more prolific when the Moon is waxing.

SILVER BIRCH SAP: collect silver birch sap when the Moon is ascending, avoiding the nodes and period (f).

PRESERVE FOOD: when the Moon is waning.

SAUERKRAUT: pick cabbages and make sauerkraut when the Moon is ascending, avoiding the same periods as for bread.

JAMS: jams with a low sugar content made when the Moon is waning will keep better.

SOURDOUGH BREAD: this will rise well and be extra delicious when the Moon is ascending. If the Moon is descending when baking, ensure that it is also waxing. Avoid nodes, the perigee, the periods (f, o, w), Water signs and constellations, if possible, and the Moon squared with the Sun and Saturn (☾ ◻ ☉ ♄) – see pages 81–11.

CLEANING AND MAINTENANCE WORK: will be more effective when the Moon is waxing.

CLOTHES: put clothes away for storage when the Moon is in conjunction with Venus (☾ ☌ ♀) – see pages 81–111.

WOODEN POSTS: to make them last longer, cut them when the Moon is new (or just before) and insert them in the ground when the Moon is in the constellation of Leo. If they are made of softwood, you can also burn the point a little to make it harder.

LAWNS: sow lawns when the Moon is waning and descending on a day favourable to 'leaf' plants or, if necessary, a 'root' date. Aerate lawns when the Moon is ascending on a 'flower' date. To help slow down growth, cut lawns when the Moon is in the constellation of Gemini and Libra or, if necessary, in Virgo or Aquarius. To promote growth, cut lawns in Pisces or, if necessary, in Cancer or Scorpio.

LIVING WITH THE MOON

Do not use the information contained in this chapter as a substitute for medical advice. If you think you have a medical problem, consult your doctor.

Influence of the phases

NEW MOON

• The renewal of physical energy is at a minimum during this phase.

• This is a good time to start eliminating toxins or to tackle a bad habit.

WAXING MOON

• We express ourselves more easily and freely.

• The body makes the most effective use of the nutrients that it receives during this phase.

• If you tend to put on weight, now is the time to do something about it.

• This is an ideal time to learn new skills or to start new projects.

FULL MOON

• Our physical energy levels are restored during this phase.

• When the nights are lighter sleep can be interrupted, and insomnia can be an issue.

• The extra energy and excitement caused by the Full Moon can be channelled into physical activities.

• Now is a good time to undertake a project.

• Some of the effects of the Full Moon and the New Moon can be felt for two or three days.

WANING MOON

• This is a good time for introspection, reflection and spirituality.

• Choose this phase to follow a detox programme; it promotes the elimination of toxins from the body.

Harvesting plants

Waxing Moon: plants harvested during the Full Moon period will have more vitality, but their medicinal properties are weaker than when the Moon is waning.

Waning Moon: plants tend to become dry but their fragrance heightens as the New Moon approaches. Plants picked during this phase will retain more of their medicinal properties.

FOR MAKING INFUSIONS

In the morning while the Moon is ascending: before midday, the Sun's influence is felt mainly on the aerial parts of a plant. It is the ideal time for harvesting leaves, flowers, fruits and seeds, and the effects are enhanced when the Moon is ascending.

In the evening while the Moon is descending: after 15:00 the Sun's influence stimulates activity in the lower parts of plants. This is the time to harvest roots. The effect is enhanced when the Moon is descending.

The following days are harmful: avoid harvesting plants when the Moon is passing through the lunar nodes when ascending or descending or when it is at its perigee (see red zones).

Colt's foot

MEDICINAL PLANTS

Harvesting flower heads (borage, St John's Wort, meadowsweet, etc.): when the Moon is waning and, if possible, also ascending, in an Air or Earth sign. Early morning is best. The following aspects are favourable: Moon conjunction, sextile or trine Sun, Venus and Mercury (☾ ♂ ✳ △ ☉ ♀ ☿) – see pages 81–111.

Borage

Harvesting roots (gentian, marsh mallow, dandelions, etc.): when the Moon is descending and, if possible, also waxing, in an Air or Earth sign. Late afternoon is best. The following aspects are favourable: Moon conjunction, sextile or trine Sun, Venus and Mercury (☾ ♂ ✳ △ ☉ ♀ ☿) – see pages 81–111.

Harvesting from trees (hawthorn, pine nuts, elderberries, etc.): when the Moon is ascending and, if possible, waxing, with the influence of a rising tide and in an Air or Earth sign. The following aspects are favourable: Moon conjunction, sextile or trine Sun, Venus and Mercury (☾ ♂ ✳ △ ☉ ♀ ☿) – see pages 81–111.

Lime blossom

Hairdressing

The table below summarizes for quick reference the best dates and times of day on which to cut hair.

■ a good day for cutting hair to **slow down hair loss**

□ a good day for cutting hair to make it **thicker and stronger**

(★) **the number of stars** indicates the strength of influence

■ **not advisable** in any circumstances. Also, to a lesser extent, it is not recommended on days marked with the sign (–)

▯ a vertical line indicates the importance of a particular part of the day. The example shows a morning favourable for reducing hair loss and a neutral afternoon

▤ days divided horizontally are favourable for the influences represented by the two colours

HAIR

	1	2	3	4	5	6	7	8	9	10	11	12	13	14	15	16	17	18	19	20	21	22	23	24	25	26	27	28	29	30	31
JANUARY						–	–	–					–									★	★		★	–★					
FEBRUARY	★	★		–	–		–											★	★		★	★							★ ★		
MARCH					–	–	–							★	★ ★	★	★	★						★	★ ★						
APRIL				–	–	–				★	★		★	★		–						★ ★	★ ★								
MAY			–	–	–			★	★	★ ★	★ ★							★	★	★											
JUNE	–	–	–	–			★		★ ★	★				–		★														★	
JULY		–	–	–	★ ★	★	★																								–
AUGUST	–	–		★															★					–		★		–	–		
SEPTEMBER	★					★															★		★ ★	★ ★	–	–	–				
OCTOBER																			★	★	★	★			–	–	–				
NOVEMBER													★	★	★	★	★					–	–	–							
DECEMBER												★ ★	★	★	★	★						★	★	–	–	–					
	1	2	3	4	5	6	7	8	9	10	11	12	13	14	15	16	17	18	19	20	21	22	23	24	25	26	27	28	29	30	31

The dates marked in this table (■, □), especially the starred ones, are highly favourable for hair. Take note of them, even if you have no particular hair problems.

- For more **manageable hair**, choose dates marked in green when the Moon is waxing.
- For a **perm**, choose the superpositions of sign and constellation ♉ ♉ (j) or ♍ ♍ (s) (see calendar pages 54–77), if possible with a waning Moon. It sets better when the Moon is waxing but the hair suffers more damage.
- Hair **coloured** when the Moon is ascending and waxing will achieve better results.
- To help hair **grow quickly**, cut it when the Moon is ascending and waxing.
- If you tend to have **split ends** and/or you want your hair to grow less quickly, we recommend that you have it cut on the following days:

am = morning   pm = afternoon

JANUARY: 1 am* - 1 pm - 2 - 3 - 4 - 5 pm - 6 am* - 22 after 15:00 - 23 - 25 after 10:00 - 26 - 27 am - 28 pm* 29 - 30 - 31 pm - **FEBRUARY:** 1 - 2 am - 2 pm* - 21 after 15h - 22 - 23 - 25 - 26 - 28 am - 29 am** - 29 pm* - **MARCH:** 22 after 10:00 - 23 pm* - 24 - 25 am** - 25 pm* - 27 - 28 before 17:00 - **APRIL:** 20 - 21 - 22 - 23 - 24 am - 24 pm* - **MAY:** 20 pm - 21 - **JULY:** 29* - 30 - **AUGUST:** 26 pm - 27 - 28 - **SEPTEMBER:** 22 - 23 - 24 - 25 am - 26 - 27 am - **OCTOBER:** 19 - 20 am - 21 - 22 am* - 23 - 24 - 25 after 10:00 - 26 - 27 pm* - **NOVEMBER:** 15 after 09:00 - 16 - 17 - 18 am - 19 - 20 pm* - 21 am - 22 - 23 - 24 - 25 - **DECEMBER:** 13 - 14 - 15 before 18:00 - 16 after 08:00 - 17 - 18 - 19 - 20 am - 20 pm* - 21 am* - 22 - 23 am - 24 - 25.

Depilation

The removal of unwanted hair is best performed when the Moon is descending; if combined with the waning Moon, regrowth will be slower. Slow down regrowth even more by choosing certain planetary aspects.

A summary indicating the best dates is shown in the table below. The dates are divided into four categories:

▢ fairly good days   ▢ good days   ▮ very good days   ★ excellent days
▮ a vertical line indicates a particular part of the day

Skincare

SKIN CLEANSING

(Blackheads, impurities, etc.) Treatment works best if carried out when the Moon is in the descendent and in an aspect with Venus (♂, ✳, ▣, △) – see pages 81–111.

NOURISHING THE SKIN

Moisten the skin with dew before applying any cream for best results. Walking barefoot in the dew is good for your general health.

- **Face packs,** moisturizing and revitalizing treatments: the right time depends on skin type.

- **Dry and combination skins:** treatments will be more effective when applied during a waxing Moon. Avoid the following signs: Aries, Cancer and Capricorn.
- **Greasy skin:** when the Moon is waning and trine and, especially, sextile with the Sun (☾ △ ✳ ☉) – see pages 81–111. The skin will absorb the products a little less well but the cleansing action will be more effective. Perform during a waning Moon to help prevent dilation of the pores, making the skin firmer and more attractive.

Warts

To remove warts with the sap from plants such as greater celandine, marigold and the fig tree...

Start when the Moon is descending, preferably during the last quarter, and when it is in the superposition of the following signs and constellations:

- Leo/Leo (♌),
- Gemini/Taurus (k)
(see pages 54–77)

Marigold

Celandine

Nails

For stronger nails, cut or file them when the Moon is waning and in an Earth or Air sign. Avoid the nodes.

Reduce the risk of in-growing nails by cutting them when the Moon is in the following signs: Leo, Virgo, Sagittarius, Capricorn and Aquarius, avoiding the lunar nodes.

Corns and callouses

Remove these when the Moon is waning and in the sign of Capricorn or Taurus. Another suitable time is when the Moon is waxing and in the sign of Virgo or Libra, though the effects are likely to be less successful.

Fasting

Fasting can be of great benefit to most people, but it is advisable to get permission from your doctor before embarking upon your first fast. Monitoring is essential for long fasts.

The New Moon is the best time to carry out a one-day fast, as your body will be cleansed more effectively. The New Moon is also a good time to begin fasts of up to a week. If you wish to fast for longer, begin when the Moon is descending and sextile with the Sun (☾ ✳ ☉) – see pages 81–111.

Detoxing

Start taking plants that help to detox your system through the liver when the Moon is in the sign of Virgo, and plants that work through the kidneys when it is in the sign of Libra. If possible, choose a time when the Moon is waning and sextile or trine with the Sun (☾ ✳ △ ☉) – see pages 81–111.

Treating worms

Carry out treatment to eradicate worms two or three days before the New Moon or, failing that, two or three days before the Full Moon.

Eating

This section is for those who have difficulty absorbing or digesting food and those wanting to derive the maximum benefit from their food.
Healthy eating involves two basic principles: moderation and intuition.

Moderation: do not overload your system by eating more than you need. Eat a varied diet made up of all the foods your body tolerates well.

Intuition: we need to learn to listen to our own body to discover what is right for it and what is not. There is no universal advice: what is right for one person is not necessarily right for another.

For example, people whose bodies tend to produce too much mucus find the condition eases if they reduce their intake of dairy products or eliminate them from their diet for a while. The problem could be a temporary one, due to tiredness or emotional stress, for example. In such instances the liver becomes overworked, and some foods, such as eggs, are less easily absorbed.

Some people have a lower tolerance for acid-producing foods. Do not confuse the acid taste of fruit such as lemons with the acidity that can

upset digestion and disturb the acid-base balance (meat, cereals). Similarly, stress, oxygen debt and lack of sleep, all of which require immediate attention, increase levels of acidity. In this case, the best solution is to eat vegetables only, except tomatoes and sorrel. Eat all other foods in moderation to avoid nutritional deficiencies, but eliminate acidic fruits from your diet.

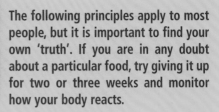

The following principles apply to most people, but it is important to find your own 'truth'. If you are in any doubt about a particular food, try giving it up for two or three weeks and monitor how your body reacts.

- Meals should be eaten in a **calm, relaxed atmosphere,** so that you can appreciate the quality of the food and the energy it provides. It is also important for your food to appeal to your senses (sight, smell and taste).
- Try to **eat less in the evening** – at the end of the day nutriments are more likely to be stored in the form of fat than used as energy.
- Meals should be taken at **regular times. Chew well** and savour them to the full.
- Avoid snacks between meals to give your **digestion a rest.**

- **Avoid** food that is **too hot or cold**: the body has to use energy to restore and maintain body temperature.
- Choose fruit and vegetables **grown organically** in your garden or organic produce free of additives (genetically modified, artificial colourings, preservatives, etc.). Their magnetic energy is greater if they are picked wet with dew. Choose **unrefined foods** (first cold-pressed oil, unrefined sugar, etc.).
- Eat fruit and vegetables **in season** and **grown locally** (their energy is best adapted to our bodies).
- Eat raw fruit **between meals**.
- Eat salad and raw vegetables at the **beginning of meals**; some people should avoid eating them in the evening.
- In winter in particular, eat **sprouting seeds** regularly; they are rich in vitamins and trace elements.

- **Seaweed** – rich in vitamins, trace elements and iodine – improves digestion when added to meals.
- **Avoid eating** meat, fish and animal by-products in the same meal.
- Some people should **avoid combining** starchy and protein foods in the same meal. Digesting them simultaneously makes conflicting demands on your stomach.

- Eat more **fibre**. Generally speaking, in affluent countries we eat too many animal products, particularly fatty foods, and insufficient fibre.
- Eat smoked products in moderation.
- Limit the amount of **preserved meats** you eat, especially if you suffer from high blood pressure, and during hot weather, when they are harder to digest.
- **Avoid** eating too many **soya beans** because of the amount of purines they contain. Leguminous plants require considerable energy to be digested.
- **Avoid oats**, which require a lot of energy to be metabolized and overheat the system. **Brown rice** is more digestible and more nourishing than white.
- If you have **kidney problems**, avoid asparagus, cress and sorrel.
- When **tired**, avoid eggs, lentils and raw pears.
- Cucumber and melon are very indigestible, especially when eaten ice-cold and with alcohol.

> **Vegetables are easier to digest and more nourishing if you cut them very thin and cook them for two or three minutes in a saucepan or wok with a little olive oil.**

The Moon influences our metabolism. If you are not lucky enough to have a cast-iron stomach, digestion and absorption will improve if you pay attention to the times when the Moon is passing through the signs and constellations (indicated by letters on the calendar on pages 54–77). Foods not mentioned below should, as a rule, be easy to digest at any time.

Digestion of the following foods demands a good deal of energy, particularly during the periods indicated by the letters (see page 12 and the calendar on pages 54–77). **Avoid eating them at these times.**

This list is not exhaustive but it applies to most foods that take a lot of time to digest. Other factors can also play a role. Stormy weather, for example, tends to hinder digestion.

Meals and the Moon

- When the Moon is waxing, nutrients are absorbed more easily.
- When the Moon is waxing and ascending, digestion requires less energy.
- People who suffer from constipation should avoid foods that contain little water (such as cereals) during Fire signs and the lunar nodes.

Beef in sauce: c-f-g-o-u-w

Mutton in sauce: d-e-f-j-r-s-u

Pork in sauce: c-d-h-o-q-s-t

Poultry in sauce: b-i-j-q-r-s-u-v-w

Preserved meats: c-d-h-i-j-L-q-r-s-t-w-x-y

Oily fish: b-c-e-f-j-k-L-o-p-y

Smoked fish: a-b-c-d-h-i-j-k-L-o-p-q-u-v-y-z

Oysters and raw shellfish: h-m-n-r-u-v-y

Eggs: f-g-i-L-m-n-q-r-u-y

Dried beans: e-j-m-n-q-r-y

Lentils: b-c-e-m-n-q-s-y

Raw celeriac: i-j-k-l-q-w-y

Raw cabbages: c-d-i-j-m-n-v-w-x

Raw cauliflowers: e-f-g-h-m-n-o-q

Cucumbers, melons: b-c-d-f-s-t-u-v-w-y-z

Radishes: a-i-j-k-q-r-s-x

Salads (curly endive, escarole): e-i-j-k-L-m-n-r-s-y-z

Raw tomatoes: b-i-m-n-o-q-r-y

Body treatments

As the Moon passes through each sign of the zodiac, certain parts of the body are stimulated (see the table on page 51). If you treat the relevant part of the body during this period, with massage, medicine, etc., you will enjoy a greater therapeutic effect.

Teeth

The table below provides a summary of the favourable and unfavourable times for dental treatment. For example, avoid having any treatment, extraction or any other operation in the upper jaw when the Moon is passing through the sign of Aries.

Similarly, avoid treatment to the teeth of the lower jaw when the Moon is passing through the sign of Taurus.

Reading the table:

▪ favourable for extracting teeth and removing nerves

▪ suitable only for extracting teeth and removing nerves from teeth in the upper jaw

▫ favourable for implants and crowns

(★) the number of stars indicates how favourable the influence is.

▪ **not advisable** under any circumstances; to a lesser extent, it is good to avoid days marked with the sign (–)

▪▏ a vertical line indicates if only a part of the day is affected – the example shows the morning as favourable for tooth extraction and the afternoon as neutral

▪ days divided horizontally are favourable for the two treatments represented by the colours

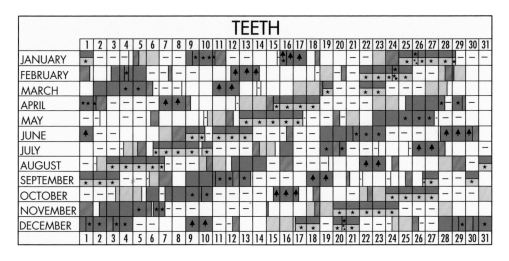

TEETH

Surgical procedures

The information below has not been validated by scientific experiment. However, it forms part of a long tradition that began with the Chaldeans and was adopted by the Egyptians, Greeks and finally, by traditional medicine in the West. It contains useful information, but it is also important to make it clear that levels of sensitivity to lunar influences vary from person to person. For example, some people suffer from sleep disturbance on nights when there is a Full Moon, while others sleep soundly. It seems that the same applies to surgical procedures and that not everyone will react in the same way.

The following information relates to operations scheduled in advance. It does not apply to emergency procedures.

As the Moon passes through the different signs of the zodiac, it stimulates different parts of the body (see the table on page 51). This makes certain treatments more effective (see page 49) but equally it can have a negative effect on surgical procedures – sometimes slowing down recovery and even causing complications, and not only in the part of the body immediately concerned.

Do not operate on any part of the body when the Moon is passing through the sign that corresponds to it exactly.

To improve the healing process and promote recovery choose a date with a waning and, if possible, an ascending Moon.

Generally, the following signs of the zodiac are favourable for surgery: Capricorn (a-b), Aquarius (c-d), Taurus (i-j), Gemini (k), Virgo (r-s) and Libra (t).

The following aspects are favourable (see pages 81–111): Moon sextile or trine Sun (☾ ✳ △ ☉), Moon conjunction, sextile or trine Venus (☾ ☌ ✳ △ ♀), Moon conjunction, sextile or trine Mercury (☾ ☌ ✳ △ ☿). Avoid the Full Moon, including the day before and the day after, as well as the New Moon and the three days following. Also avoid lunar nodes, the perigee and the Moon square with Saturn or the Sun. For successful surgery involving the skin (cosmetic surgery), see the recommendations for surgery (above) and also choose a descending Moon with the influence of a rising tide.

The above information is far from complete, but its aim is simply to raise awareness of this traditional belief. For further study of the subject, consult experts in the field or specialist books. Be sure to always take any medical prescriptions or instructions into account.

The body and the zodiac

This table shows the correlation between the signs of the zodiac and different parts of the body.

ARIES	skull, brain, upper jaw, face, facial muscles, eyes
TAURUS	throat, neck, lips, palate, larynx, tonsils, tongue, ears, cerebellum, neck vertebrae, thyroid, lower jaw
GEMINI	upper limbs, hands, lungs, bronchial tubes, respiratory tracts, nervous system, capillaries
CANCER	oesophagus, stomach, ribs, breastbone, upper lobes of the liver, pancreas, breasts, diaphragm
LEO	heart, solar plexus, aorta, back vertebrae, spinal cord
VIRGO	abdominal region, duodenum, spleen, lower lobe of the liver, small intestine, large intestine
LIBRA	kidneys, adrenal glands, ureters, lumbar region, skin
SCORPIO	bladder, urethra, genital organs, prostate, descending colon, rectum, nose, pubis
SAGITTARIUS	hips, pelvis, coccyx, sacrum, thigh bones, ischium and iliac bone (hip), the sciatic nerve, femoral artery, saphena veins
CAPRICORN	knees, knee caps, cartilage, skin, nails, hair, bones in general
AQUARIUS	leg, tibia, fibula, ankle, Achilles' tendon
PISCES	feet, toes, lymphatic circulation

Understanding the calendar

On the calendar on pages 54–77, the phases of the Moon (New Moon ●, first quarter ◐, last quarter ◑, Full Moon ○) as well as its perigee P and its apogee A, are represented in the top band.

The band beneath shows the Chinese seasons and inter-seasonal periods. Beneath these are the bands indicating the signs and constellations of the zodiac, each of which is illustrated by a coloured strip that corresponds to the four elements:

FIRE	EARTH	AIR	WATER

The letters between these bands indicate where signs and constellations can be used in conjunction (see page 12).

The curve of the coloured bands represents the Moon ascending and descending and the black triangles indicate when the change occurs. When the bands curve upwards, the Moon is ascending and vice versa. This movement is also reflected by the thin coloured bands beneath the wider blue band with the dates – green for the ascending Moon and yellow for the descending Moon.

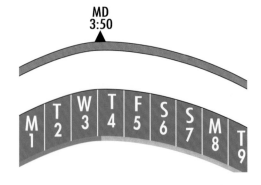

Cultivating the soil (particularly at depth), planting (for example, trees), planting out (especially plants with bare roots) and spreading compost or manure should be carried out when the Moon is descending, which is the best time for plants to take root.

The signs, letters and numbers in the white band are relevant to harvesting. The length of time is indicated by the vertical lines.

Ascending Moon:
harvest aerial parts of plant (green stars)
Descending Moon:
harvest parts of plant below ground (yellow stars)

The period for sowing different plants is indicated by the green band, which is in parallel with the constellations. The time when work should be carried out depends on why the plant is being grown (for its fruits, roots, flowers or leaves), avoiding the red zones. For example, choose a date favourable to 'leaf' plants for houseplants that do not flower and a 'flower' date for plants that do. Another example is to sow endives on 'root' dates and force their growth on 'leaf' dates.

The white band completes the information given in the green band. A summary of all the lunar and planetary effects on crops is given by indicating various zones ranging from 'harmful' (red band) to 'very favourable' (∗∗∗) and also 'to be avoided' (—). Use these symbols in conjunction with the green band above for a clear and comprehensive understanding.

All the times mentioned are Greenwich Mean Time or British Summer Time, as appropriate. For other countries, see page 2.
Cut out the detachable page giving instructions on how best to use the calendar and use it as a bookmark to remind you to use the calendar every month.

JANUARY

SIGNS OF THE ZODIAC

| ♈ ARIES | ♌ LEO | ♐ SAGITTARIUS | ♉ TAURUS | ♍ VIRGO | ♑ CAPRICORN | ♊ GEMINI | ♎ LIBRA | ♒ AQUARIUS | ♋ CANCER | ♏ SCORPIO | ♓ PISCES |

CONSTELLATIONS

3 January: the Earth is at its closest to the Sun (the perihelion) – about 147 million km (92 million miles).

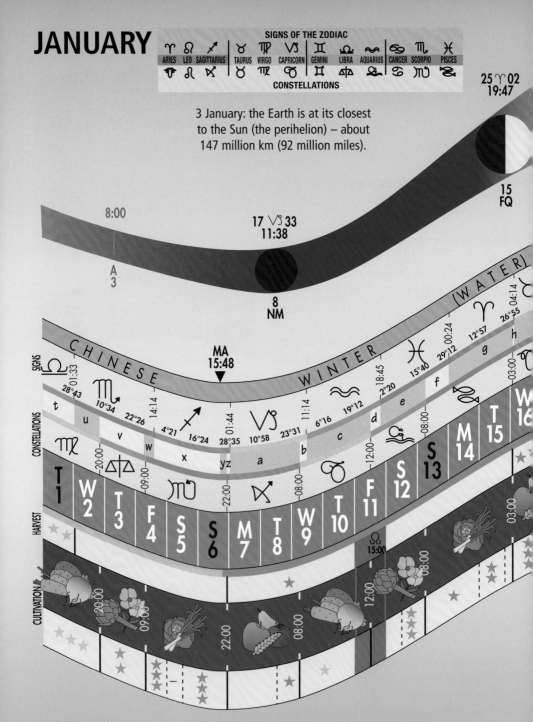

To help you make full use of the calendar, activities are suggested for each month.

09:00

1 ♌ 54
13:36

18 January: the Sun enters the constellation of Capricorn.

20 January: the Sun enters the sign of Aquarius at 16:45.

P
19

22
FM

9 ♏ 40
05:04

04:00

MD
23:29

30
LQ

A
31

INTER-SEASON

(EARTH)

♉ 06:31
25°28

♊
9°58 24°30 08:06

♋
8°58 23°17 10:21

♌
7°22 21°07 14:49

♍
17°32 22:36
4°31

♎
0°12 12°33 24°42 09:36

♏
6°39 18°32

↗
0°24 22:09

°06

i   j   k   Lm   n   o   p   q   r   s   t   u   v   w   x

♉
19:00

07:00

♊
06:00

♋
18:00

♌

♍

♎

♏

♐

18:00

10:00

T
17

F
18

S
19

S
20

M
21

T
22

W
23

T
24

F
25

S
26

S
27

M
28

T
29

W
30

T
31

F
1

P
09:00

♒
11:00

♏
04:00

♑
17:00

19:00

07:00

06:00

18:00

10:00

04:00

17:00

Cutting wood: see page 37.
Pruning: see pages 22–24.

The colours of the stars relate to different types of plants (for example, red = fruit plants).

Note: all times given are in Greenwich Mean Time.

FEBRUARY

7 February:
Chinese New Year.

15 February: the Sun
enters the constellation
of Aquarius.

24 ♉ 49
03:35
01:00

14
FQ

P
14

17 ≈ 44
03:46

7
NM

C H I N E S E

MA
23:31
▼

♐
12°22 24°27 09:53 6°44 19°16

♑
2°03 19:11 15°06 28°26 01:47 12°00 25°46 06:18 9°42 23°46 7°55 22°06 09:35 01:00 6°18 12:20

♓

♒

♈ ♉ ♊

SIGNS

♎

♋

CONSTELLATIONS

♍♌   ♐
06:00

x   yz   a   b   c   d   e   f   g   h   i   j   k

16:00   19:00   15:00   08:00   01:00

| F 1 | S 2 | S 3 | M 4 | T 5 | W 6 | T 7 | F 8 | S 9 | S 10 | M 11 | T 12 | W 13 | T 14 | F 15 |

P
01:00

HARVEST

♋
22:00

★   ★   ★   ★ ★   ★   ★ ★

19:00   15:00   08:00

★★   ★★   ★★★

CULTIVATION

06:00   16:00

—   ★   ★ ★   ★   ★   ★   ★   ★★   ★★

Cereal crops: see page 31.

Hair care and depilation: see pages 42–43.

Eclipses on 7 and 21 February: see page 9.

SIGNS OF THE ZODIAC

♈	♌	♐	♉	♍	♑	♊	♎	♒	♋	♏	♓
ARIES	LEO	SAGITTARIUS	TAURUS	VIRGO	CAPRICORN	GEMINI	LIBRA	AQUARIUS	CANCER	SCORPIO	PISCES

CONSTELLATIONS

1 ♍ 53
03:32

19 February: the Sun
enters the sign of
Pisces at 06:51.

21
FM

9 ♐ 52
02:19

01:00

A
28

29
LQ

S P R I N G

15:13

69

4°33   18:32

18:52

♌

2°22   15:59   00:07

♍

29°22   12:30

25°22   07:46

[W O O D]

♎

7°58   20°18   18:07

2°27

14°26   26°20   06:23

♏

8°13   20°09

18:34

MA
08:01
▼

m

n

o

p

q

r

s

t

u

v

w

x   y z

14:00

14:00

14:00

03:00

19:00

13:00

01:00

15:00

♊

♋

♍

♏

♑

S 16	S 17	M 18	T 19	W 20	T 21	F 22	S 23	S 24	M 25	T 26	W 27	T 28	F 29	S 1

20:00

14:00

03:00

19:00

19:00

13:00

01:00

15:00

All the advice on the
calendar also applies to **the
southern hemisphere**, except for
the inversion of the ascending and
descending Moon (see page 6).

Note: all times given are in Greenwich Mean Time.

MARCH

11 March: the Sun enters the constellation of Pisces.

24 ♊ 14
10:47

17 ♓ 31
17:15

22:00

14
FQ

MD
11:33

P
10

7
NM

MA
08:01

C H I N E S E

17:55
3°03
17°18
1°22
15°13

16:15
18°37

14:24
19°34
4°05
5°07
20°53
6°55
23:17
10°01
04:26
27°06
14°32
2°15
18:34

15:00
07:00
19:00
15:00

k   L m   n

♉   ♊

j

i
h
g
f
e
d
c
b
a
y z

SIGNS

CONSTELLATIONS

HARVEST

CULTIVATION

S 1 | S 2 | M 3 | T 4 | W 5 | T 6 | F 7 | S 8 | S 9 | M 10 | T 11 | W 12 | T 13 | F 14 | S 15 | S 16

07:00
04:00
23:00
22:00
15:00
07:00
19:00
01:00
04:00
01:00
15:00

March is a good month for **pruning** apple trees, but do not leave it any later.

Prune when the Moon is descending, for example 15–28 March. See page 23.

To prevent onions and shallots from going to seed, plant them on a day favourable to 'root' plants when the Moon is descending, such as 22–24 March. When planting asparagus crowns, wait for a 'leaf' date when the Moon is descending, such as 27–28 March.

SIGNS OF THE ZODIAC

| ♈ ARIES | ♌ LEO | ♐ SAGITTARIUS | ♉ TAURUS | ♍ VIRGO | ♑ CAPRICORN | ♊ GEMINI | ♎ LIBRA | ♒ AQUARIUS | ♋ CANCER | ♏ SCORPIO | ♓ PISCES |

CONSTELLATIONS

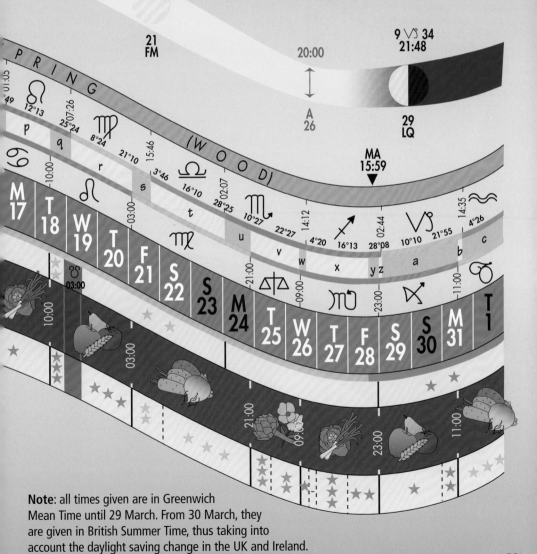

20 March: the Sun enters the sign of Aries at 05:49 (Vernal equinox).

01♎31 18:41

21 FM

9♑34 21:48

20:00

A 26

29 LQ

MA 15:59 ▼

SPRING (WOOD)

Note: all times given are in Greenwich Mean Time until 29 March. From 30 March, they are given in British Summer Time, thus taking into account the daylight saving change in the UK and Ireland.

APRIL

6 April: the beginning of the Red Moon.

Green manure: while waiting for the next food crop to grow, sow green manure to protect and enrich the soil (clover, phacelia, mustard, cereals with vetch or peas, buckwheat and spinach). Sow on a date favourable to 'leaf' plants to achieve abundant growth or, better still, a 'roots' date for maximum improvement to the structure of the soil.

For plants that easily go to seed (lettuces, onions and so on), look for the appropriate constellation with the Moon in the descendent. For instance, 23–24 April for lettuces. 1 April is a good day for planting potatoes.

SIGNS OF THE ZODIAC

♈	♌	♐	♉	♍	♑	♊	♎	♒	♋	♏	♓
ARIES	LEO	SAGITTARIUS	TAURUS	VIRGO	CAPRICORN	GEMINI	LIBRA	AQUARIUS	CANCER	SCORPIO	PISCES

CONSTELLATIONS

18 April: the Sun enters the constellation of Aries.

19 April: the Sun enters the sign of Taurus at 17:52.

0 ♏ 43
11:26

8 ♒ 39
15:13

11:00

20
FM

28
LQ

A
23

INTER-SEASON (EARTH)

MA
23:34

Grafting: see page 24.
Weeds: see page 29.

Note: all times given are in British Summer Time.

MAY

5 May: end of the Red Moon.

When sowing, always choose the constellation that suits the type of plant, if possible when there is the maximum number of stars. For example, 2–3 May for leeks, 19 May for flowers. Always avoid the red zones and, as far as possible, days marked with the sign (—).

Note: all times given are in British Summer Time.

SIGNS OF THE ZODIAC

♈	♌	♐	♉	♍	♑	♊	♎	♒	♋	♏	♓
ARIES	LEO	SAGITTARIUS	TAURUS	VIRGO	CAPRICORN	GEMINI	LIBRA	AQUARIUS	CANCER	SCORPIO	PISCES

CONSTELLATIONS

13 May: the Sun enters the constellation of Taurus.

20 May: the Sun enters the sign of Gemini at 17:02.

7 ♓ 10
03:58

29 ♏ 27
03:12

15:00

28
LQ

20
FM A
     20

[FIRE]

MA
04:58

SUMMER

A good day for **sowing root vegetables**: 25 May. The day indicated for **pricking out salad vegetables**: 21 May.

63

JUNE

SIGNS OF THE ZODIAC

♈	♌	♐	♉	♍	♑	♊	♎	♒	♋	♏	♓
ARIES	LEO	SAGITTARIUS	TAURUS	VIRGO	CAPRICORN	GEMINI	LIBRA	AQUARIUS	CANCER	SCORPIO	PISCES

CONSTELLATIONS

13 ♊ 34
20:24
14:00

20 ♍ 06
16:05

P 3
3 NM

MD
12:35

10
FQ

SIGNS

23:20
14°44
i
29°56 j
15°14 k
Lm
0°26
23:07
22:17
15:24
29°59
n
o
14°05
27°44
p
03:02
23:01
q
r
C H I N E S E
♍ 10°56
23:45
10:56
s
6°14
18°28
t
21°54
0°33
u
v
12:30

CONSTELLATIONS

12:00
21:00
18:00
07:00
22:00
17:00

S 1
M 2
T 3
W 4
T 5
F 6
S 7
S 8
M 9
T 10
W 11
T 12
F 13
S 14
S 15

HARVEST

P 14:00
★ ★
★ ★
♉ 10:00
★
♍
⚖

CULTIVATION

★ ★
★ ★
★
★ ★ ★
★ ★
★
★

To ensure grass grows back more slowly,
cut it on a date favourable to 'flower' plants or, if
that is not possible, when the Moon is descending,
for instance 5, 6, 11, 12, 13, 14 June.

Hay: see page 30.

Note: all times given are in British Summer Time.

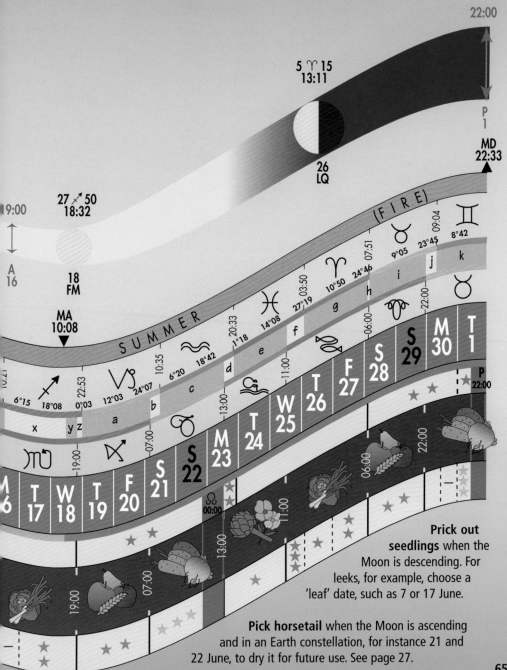

20 June: the Sun enters the constellation of Gemini.

21 June: the Sun enters the sign of Cancer at 01:00 (Summer solstice).

5 ♈ 15
13:11

26
LQ

22:00

P
1

MD
22:33

27 ♐ 50
18:32

9:00

A
16

18
FM

MA
10:08

(F I R E)

♊
8°42

k

♉

♉
23°45 09:04

j

9°05

i

07:51

h

24°46 07:07

♈
10°50

g

14°08 03:19

♓
27°19

f

20:33

e

1°18

d

18°42 10:35

♑
12°03 24°07

c

6°20

b

22:53

0°03

a

♋

6°15 18°08

19:00

♐

x   y z

♍

SUMMER

M
16

T
17

W
18

T
19

F
20

S
21

S
22

M
23

T
24

W
25

T
26

F
27

S
28

S
29

M
30

T
1

P
22:00

♌
00:00

Prick out seedlings when the Moon is descending. For leeks, for example, choose a 'leaf' date, such as 7 or 17 June.

Pick horsetail when the Moon is ascending and in an Earth constellation, for instance 21 and 22 June, to dry it for future use. See page 27.

JULY

22:00 11 ♋ 32
03:20

4 July: the earth is at its furthest from the Sun (its aphelion) – about 152 million km (95 million miles).

P 1 — 3 NM

18 ♎ 18
05:36

MD 22:33

10 FQ

05:00

A 14

MA 16:04

SIGNS · CONSTELLATIONS · HARVEST · CULTIVATION

CHINESE SUMMER

(FIRE

The morning of 6 July is a good time for separating and **planting strawberry runners**.

Note: all times given are in British Summer Time.

19 July: the Sun enters the constellation of Cancer.

22 July: the Sun enters the sign of Leo at 11:56.

Water plants more during dry periods – to ensure roots grow deep, water generously but less often, rather than little and often. To avoid water evaporating too quickly, hoe the ground a few hours after watering, if possible in the evening with a waxing Moon in an Earth or Water sign, e.g. 3, 6, 7, 8, 11, 12, 16, 17 July.

9 ♌ 32
11:14

1
NM

SIGNS OF THE ZODIAC

♈	♌	♐	♉	♍	♑	♊	♎	♒	♋	♏	♓
ARIES	LEO	SAGITTARIUS	TAURUS	VIRGO	CAPRICORN	GEMINI	LIBRA	AQUARIUS	CANCER	SCORPIO	PISCES
♈	♌	♐	♉	♍	♑	♊	♎	♒	♋	♏	♓

CONSTELLATIONS

10 August: the Sun enters the
constellation of Leo.

16 ♏ 38
21:21

21:00

8
FQ

A
10

SIGNS

INTER-SEASON (EARTH)

♌
16°32

22:00

♍
0°33

14°14

27°32 03:29

♎
10°28

23°04

12:27

♏
17°27

5°22

00:11

29°24

MA
23:14

CHINESE

♐
11°17

23:11

♑
5°08

17°13

29°30

23:57

12°00

≈

CONSTELLATIONS

♋

02:00

p

q

r

♌

s

t

u

♍

v

w

x

y z

♒

a

b

c

HARVEST

F
1

S
2

S
3

M
4

♍
T
5

W
6

T
7

♎
F
8

S
9

S
10

♏
M
11

T
12

W
13

♐
T
14

F
15

♉
S
16

02:00

07:00

19:00

09:00

20:00

CULTIVATION

02:00

15:00

15:00

07:00

19:00

09:00

20:00

11:

Note: all times given are in British Summer Time.

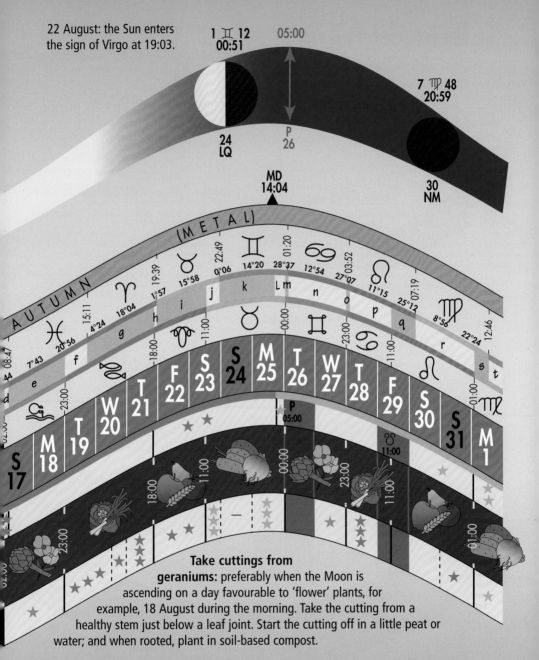

22 August: the Sun enters the sign of Virgo at 19:03.

Take cuttings from geraniums: preferably when the Moon is ascending on a day favourable to 'flower' plants, for example, 18 August during the morning. Take the cutting from a healthy stem just below a leaf joint. Start the cutting off in a little peat or water; and when rooted, plant in soil-based compost.

Disbud chrysanthemums when the Moon is in the sign of Libra, for example 8–9 August.

Eclipses on 1 and 16 August: see page 9.

Shield budding: see page 24.

SEPTEMBER

SIGNS OF THE ZODIAC

♈	♌	♐	♉	♍	♑	♊	♎	♒	♋	♏	♓
ARIES	LEO	SAGITTARIUS	TAURUS	VIRGO	CAPRICORN	GEMINI	LIBRA	AQUARIUS	CANCER	SCORPIO	PISCES

CONSTELLATIONS

15 September: the Sun enters the
constellation of Virgo.

22 ♓ 54
10:14

15 ♐ 19
15:05
16:00

15
FM

7 A
FQ 7

Cereal crops: see page 31.

Harvesting grapes: see page 35.

70

22 September: the Sun enters
the sign of Libra at 16:46.
(Autumnal equinox)

Compost: apply compost on one of the dates given on page 26.
Wait for the a descending Moon before applying.
For **spreading manure**: see page 26.

Preserving fruit: take account of the 'harvest' band when picking fruit and also of the
information on page 25.

Note: all times given are in British Summer Time.

OCTOBER

SIGNS OF THE ZODIAC

♈	♌	♐		♉	♍	♑		♊	♎	♒		♋	♏	♓
ARIES	LEO	SAGITTARIUS		TAURUS	VIRGO	CAPRICORN		GEMINI	LIBRA	AQUARIUS		CANCER	SCORPIO	PISCES

CONSTELLATIONS

21 ♈ 51
21:04

14
FM

14 ♑ 28
10:05

12:00

7
FQ

A
5

MA
15:05

AUTUMN

SIGNS

CHINESE

CONSTELLATIONS

HARVEST

CULTIVATION

72

23 October: the Sun enters the sign of Scorpio at 02:10.

31 October: the Sun enters the constellation of Libra.

07:00

28 ⬡ 27
12:56

P
17

21
LQ

MD
01:19

[M E T A L]

5 ♏ 54
23:15

11:26   ♊   12:41

2°20   7°05   21°43   6°09   20°21   15:36   4°15   17°53   20:41   1°17   ♍   14°27   02:49   27°25   ♎   23°20   11:48   5°46   ♏   18°02   22:42   0°09   12°06

♋

♌

I N T E R - S E A S O N (E A R T H)

j   k   L m   n   o   p   q   r   s   t   u   v   w   x

29
NM

MA
20:55

00:00   ♉   11:00   ♊   11:00   ♋   12:00   ♌   15:00   ♎   10°44   ♏   ♐

F
17

S
18

S
19

M
20

T
21

W
22

T
23

F
24

S
25

S
26

M
27

T
28

W
29

T
30

F
31

S
1

P
07:00

★   ★★   ⊗
19:00

★   ★★   ★

★

★★   ★

★

12:00   11:00   11:00   12:00   13:00   15:00   07:00   18:00

07:00   18:00

Note: all times given are in British Summer Time until 25 October and GMT from 26 October.

Take cuttings on 18 October (end of the ascending Moon) and plant them in the ground on 19 October (beginning of the descending Moon), see page 24.

21 ♉ 15 10:00
06:18

13
FM

P
14

MD
08:19

14 ♒ 07
04:04

05:00

6
FQ

CHINESE

19:53

♊

20:12
16:54

1°45

♉
19:00

16:40
i j k L m

1°46
h

20:06

17:15
g

3°11
17:27
♈

MA
20:55

INTER-SEASON (EARTH)

A
2

10:44
19:36
♓
f

6°31
e

23:51

11:32
d

00:03

29°28
c

♑
17:34
b

5°46

11:14
23:58

♐
x y z a

♑
08:00

20:00

♐

03:00
01:00

04:00

♎
04:00

01:00

SIGNS

S
1

S
2

M
3

T
4

W
5

T
6

F
7

S
8

S
9

M
10

T
11

W
12

T
13

F
14

S
15

P
10:00

19:00

CONSTELLATIONS

19:00

09:00

HARVEST

20:00

03:00

08:00

CULTIVATION

Note: all times given are in
Greenwich Mean Time.

Timber: cut timber on the dates marked on page 37 to
benefit from the lunar influences, if possible during November
and December to benefit from the descending Sun as well.

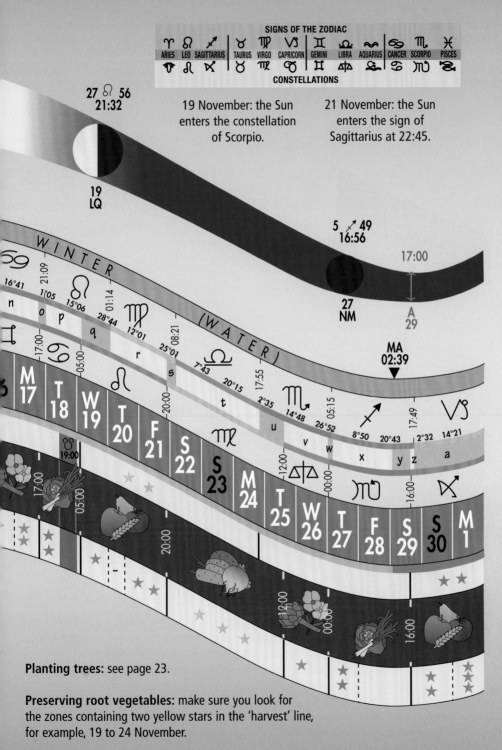

SIGNS OF THE ZODIAC

♈	♌	♐	♉	♍	♑	♊	♎	♒	♋	♏	♓
ARIES	LEO	SAGITTARIUS	TAURUS	VIRGO	CAPRICORN	GEMINI	LIBRA	AQUARIUS	CANCER	SCORPIO	PISCES

CONSTELLATIONS

27 ♌ 56
21:32

19 November: the Sun enters the constellation of Scorpio.

21 November: the Sun enters the sign of Sagittarius at 22:45.

19
LQ

5 ♐ 49
16:56

17:00

27
NM

A
29

MA
02:39
▼

W I N T E R

16°41   21:09   1:05
15°06   01:14
28°44   12°01   ♍
25°08:21

(W A T E R)

7°43   17.55
20°15   2°35
14°48   05:15
26°52   8°50   20°43   17:49   2°32   14°21

♎   ♏   ♐   ♑

n   o   p   q   r   s   t   u   v   w   x   y   z   a

| M 17 | T 18 | W 19 | T 20 | F 21 | S 22 | S 23 | M 24 | T 25 | W 26 | T 27 | F 28 | S 29 | S 30 | M 1 |

19:00   17:00   05:00   20:00   12:00   00:00   16:00

Planting trees: see page 23.

Preserving root vegetables: make sure you look for the zones containing two yellow stars in the 'harvest' line, for example, 19 to 24 November.

DECEMBER

21 ♊ 02
16:38
22:00

14 ♓ 08
21:27

12 P
FM 12

MD
18:39

5
FQ

CHINESE

The period between Christmas and Epiphany is a good time for people to **reflect and take stock**. You can also make use of this time to try and predict what the weather will be like during the next 12 months. Make a very precise note at fixed hours several times a day of what the weather is like between 24 December and 6 January. In theory, the weather in January will correspond to the weather as it was on 24/25 December, the weather in February to the weather conditions on 25/26 December and so on. Keep 24/25 December as your starting point. Try it and see if it works.

SIGNS OF THE ZODIAC

| ♈ ARIES | ♌ LEO | ♐ SAGITTARIUS | ♉ TAURUS | ♍ VIRGO | ♑ CAPRICORN | ♊ GEMINI | ♎ LIBRA | ♒ AQUARIUS | ♋ CANCER | ♏ SCORPIO | ♓ PISCES |

CONSTELLATIONS

19 December: the Sun enters the constellation of Sagittarius.

21 December: the Sun enters the sign of Capricorn at 12:05.

27 ♍ 54
10:30

19
LQ

6 ♑ 08
12:23
18:00

27
NM
A
26

WINTER

(WATER)
MA
08:00

Cut **firewood** when the Moon is descending from 13 to 25 December.
For timber: see page 37.

Companion planting

Plants release secretions into the soil via their roots so one plant can affect the growth of another nearby. The Chinese and the South American Indians have known about this and made good use of the knowledge for centuries. Organizing your garden so that you position those plants that have a beneficial effect on each other side by side is another way to help improve your gardening success. Try your own companion planting experiments; results will vary according to the type of soil.

Plant	Grows well with	Does not grow well with
Asparagus	Cucumber, leek, parsley, pea, tomato	Beetroot, garlic, onion
Aubergine	French bean	Potato
Beetroot	Cabbage, celery, lettuce, onion	Asparagus, carrot, leek, runner bean, tomato
Cabbage (except kohlrabi)	Beetroot, celery, corn salad, French bean, lettuce, onion, pea, potato, tomato	Chicory, fennel, garlic, leek, parsnip, radish
Carrot	Chervil, chive, dwarf French bean, lettuce, onion, leek, parsley, parsnip, pea, radish, tomato	Beetroot, Swiss chard
Celery	Beetroot, cabbage, cucurbitaceous plants, French bean, leek, pea, Swiss chard, tomato	Lettuce, maize, parsley
Chicory		Cabbage
Corn salad	Cabbage, leek, onion, strawberry	
Cucumber	Asparagus, basil, cabbage, celery, chive, French bean, lettuce, maize, pea	Potato, radish, tomato
Fennel	Celery, leek	Cabbage, French bean, parsnip, tomato
French bean	Aubergine, carrot, celery, cabbage, lettuce, maize, marigold, potato, spinach, radish, strawberry, turnip	Beetroot, garlic, fennel, onion, shallot, Swiss chard
Garlic	Potato, strawberry	Cabbage, French bean, marigold, pea

Plant	Grows well with	Does not grow well with
Kohlrabi	Beetroot, celery, leek, lettuce	Chicory, fennel, radish, strawberry
Leek	Asparagus, carrot, celery, fennel, lettuce, onion, strawberry, tomato	Beetroot, cabbage, parsley, pea, Swiss chard
Lettuce	Beetroot, cabbage, carrot, chervil, cucumber, broad bean, leek, onion, pea, strawberry, radish, turnip	Parsley
Maize	Cucurbitaceous plants, French beans, pea, potato, tomato	Beetroot, celery
Marrow and courgette	Basil, maize, nasturtium, potato	Potato, radish
Onion	Beetroot, carrot, cucumber, leek, lettuce, parsley, parsnip, strawberry, tomato	Cabbage, French bean, pea, potato
Parsnip	Carrot, onion	Fennel
Pea	Asparagus, cabbage, carrot, celery, cucumber, lettuce, maize, potato, radish, turnip	Garlic, leek, onion, parsley, shallot
Potato	Broad bean, cabbage, celery, French bean, garlic, marigold, nasturtium, pea, tomato	Aubergine, cucumber, maize, onion
Radish	Carrot, chervil, French bean, garlic, lettuce, pea, spinach, tomato	Cabbage, marrow
Spinach	Cabbage, French bean, radish, strawberry, turnip	Beetroot, Swiss chard
Strawberry	Chive, corn salad, French bean, garlic, leek, lettuce, marigold, onion, spinach, thyme, turnip	Cabbage
Swiss chard	Celery, lettuce, onion	Asparagus, basil, leek, tomato
Tomato	Asparagus, basil, carrot, garlic, cabbage, celery, leek, French marigold, nasturtium, marigold, onion, parsley, parsnip, potato, radish	Beetroot, fennel, kohlrabi, pea, Swiss chard
Turnip	French bean, lettuce, pea, spinach	

Index

JANUARY

		Times of the tides	Ascending and descending moon, and moon phases	Constellations (gardening)	Times of moon rising and setting	Compost	Insecticides Fungicides	Winegrowing	Wood	Hair	Depilation				☉ SUN	☿ MERCURY	♀ VENUS	♂ MARS	♃ JUPITER	♄ SATURN	♅ URANUS	♆ NEPTUNE	♇ PLUTO
T	1	2:15 / 7:30 / 12:30 / 19:45			1:17 / 11:29		I / F	▯	⚒		▮					☿ 2							△ 6	
W	2	3:30 / 8:15 / 12:45 / 20:30			2:28 / 11:42		I / F	▯	⚒		▮							△ 1	⚹ 8	⚹ 19			⚹ 0
T	3	4:45 / 9:00 / 13:00 / 21:15	A 8:00		3:41 / 12:00		I	▯	⚒		▮				☉ ⚹ 2						△ 9	19	
F	4	6:00 / 9:45 / 13:30 / 22:00			4:53 / 12:23		I	▯	⚒		▮					☿ ⚹ 1							
S	5	7:00 / 10:30 / 14:00 / 23:00			6:03 / 12:55			▯	⚒	✂	▮						♀ ☌ 3			♄ 7	♅ 21		
S	6	8:00 / 11:30 / 14:45 / 23:45			7:06 / 13:40			▯	⚒	✂	▮							♂ ☌ 22				⚹ 7	
M	7	9:00 / 12:15 / 15:45			7:57 / 14:39		F	▯		—									♃ ☌ 10	♄ △ 18			☌ 0
T	8	0:45 / 9:30 / 13:15 / 16:45	●		8:36 / 15:50		✚		—					☉ ☌ 12						♅ ⚹ 8		
W	9	1:30 / 10:00 / 14:00 / 18:15			9:04 / 17:08	C	✚	🏠	—						☿ ☌ 16							
T	10	2:30 / 10:30 / 14:45 / 19:30			9:25 / 18:28	C	✚	🏠								♀ ⚹ 12						
F	11	3:15 / 10:45 / 15:45 / 20:45	☍ 15:00		9:41 / 19:49			🏠									♂ △ 12				♆ ☌ 2	⚹ 18
S	12	4:00 / 11:00 / 16:30 / 22:15			9:54 / 21:08	C	✚	🏠										♃ ⚹ 5	♄ ☍ 9	♅ ☌ 23		
S	13	4:45 / 11:00 / 17:15 / 23:30			10:07 / 22:29		✚	🏠	—					☉ ⚹ 11		♀ 0	♂ 17					
M	14	5:30 / 11:15 / 18:00			10:19 / 23:51		✚								☿ ⚹ 19			♃ 11				☌ 0
T	15	0:45 / 6:15 / 11:30 / 18:45	◑		10:33		✚							☉ 20		♀ △ 9	♂ ⚹ 21				⚹ 12	

81

JANUARY

Day	Times of the tides	Ascending/descending moon, moon phases	Constellations	Times of moon rising and setting	Compost	Insecticides Fungicides	Winegrowing	Wood	Hair	Depilation	SUN	MERCURY	VENUS	MARS	JUPITER	SATURN	URANUS	NEPTUNE	PLUTO
W 16	2:15 / 7:15 / 11:45 / 19:30			1:16 / 10:50			✚	🏠	✂						Δ15	Δ18			Δ4
T 17	3:45 / 8:00 / 12:15 / 20:30			2:44 / 11:12			✚	🏠	✂			4					✳7	15	
F 18	5:15 / 9:00 / 12:45 / 21:30			4:13 / 11:44	C		✚	🏠			Δ2					19			
S 19	6:30 / 10:00 / 13:30 / 22:30	P 9:00		5:35 / 12:31	C		✚	🏠				Δ11	☌23				9	Δ17	
S 20	7:45 / 11:15 / 14:30 / 23:45			6:44 / 13:37	C			⚒	⟋					☌0	☌21	✳21			☌8
M 21	8:30 / 12:15 / 16:00			7:33 / 14:58	C			⚒	⟋								Δ11		
T 22	0:45 / 9:00 / 13:15 / 17:30	◯		8:07 / 16:25			🍾	⚒	✂	⟋	☌14								
W 23	1:45 / 9:30 / 14:00 / 18:45	☊☿ 2:00		8:30 / 17:51			🍾	⚒	✂	⟋								☌23	
T 24	2:30 / 9:45 / 15:00 / 20:15	☍ 11:00		8:47 / 19:13				⚒		⟋		☌0	Δ15	✳5					Δ15
F 25	3:15 / 10:00 / 15:45 / 21:30			9:01 / 20:31		F	🍾	⚒	✂	⟋					Δ6	☌4	☌21		
S 26	4:00 / 10:15 / 16:15 / 22:45			9:12 / 21:46		F	🍾	⚒	—	⟋				12					23
S 27	4:45 / 10:30 / 17:00			9:23 / 22:59		I / F	🍾	⚒		⟋	Δ12		5		16				
M 28	0:00 / 5:30 / 10:30 / 17:45			9:35		I / F	🍾	⚒		⟋		Δ21		Δ22				Δ16	
T 29	1:15 / 6:00 / 10:45 / 18:30			0:12 / 9:48	C	I / F	🍾	⚒		⟋									✳10
W 30	2:30 / 6:45 / 11:00 / 19:15	◑		1:24 / 10:03		I	🍾	⚒		⟋	5		✳0		✳5	✳0	Δ19		

FEBRUARY — page 84

Day	Times of the tides	Asc/desc moon, moon phases	Constellations (gardening)	Times of moon rising and setting	Compost	Insecticides Fungicides	Winegrowing	Wood	Hair	Depilation	SUN ☉	MERCURY ☿	VENUS ♀	MARS ♂	JUPITER ♃	SATURN ♄	URANUS ♅	NEPTUNE ♆	PLUTO ♇
S 17	6:30 / 10:00 / 13:30 / 22:30			5:29 / 12:36	C			↗		∥					♃☌14	♄✳1	♅△21		
M 18	7:00 / 11:00 / 15:00 / 23:30			6:07 / 13:59	C			↗		∥				♀☌21					
T 19	7:30 / 12:00 / 16:30			6:33 / 15:25				↗ ✂		∥			☿☌9						
W 20	0:15 / 7:45 / 12:45 / 17:45	☿20:00		6:52 / 16:48				↗ ✂		∥				♂✳18				♆☌10	
T 21	1:00 / 8:00 / 13:30 / 19:15	○		7:07 / 18:08	F	🍷		↗ ✂		∥	☉☌4					♄☌10			♇△1
F 22	1:45 / 8:15 / 14:15 / 20:30			7:19 / 19:24	F	🍷		↗ ✂		∥					♃△2		♅☌9		
S 23	2:30 / 8:30 / 15:00 / 21:45			7:30 / 20:38	I / F	🍷		↗		∥				♀△23 ♂□2					♇9
S 24	3:15 / 8:45 / 15:45 / 22:45			7:41 / 21:52	I / F	🍷		↗		∥			☿△2		♃12				
M 25	4:00 / 9:00 / 16:15			7:54 / 23:05	C / I / F	🍷		↗		∥				♂△14				♆△3	♇✳20
T 26	0:00 / 4:45 / 9:15 / 17:00			8:08	I	🍷		↗		∥	☉△8	☿16	♀16			♄✳4			
W 27	1:15 / 5:30 / 9:30 / 17:45			0:19 / 8:27	I	🍷		↗		∥					♃✳0		♅△6	♆15	
T 28	2:30 / 6:15 / 9:45 / 18:45	A 1:00		1:32 / 8:51		🍷		↗ ✂		∥						♄16			
F 29	3:45 / 7:00 / 10:30 / 19:30	◑		2:40 / 9:25		🍷		↗ ✂		∥	☉2	☿✳9	♀✳12				♅19		

MARCH

	Times of the tides	Ascending and descending moon, and moon phases	Constellations (gardening)	Times of moon rising and setting	Compost	Insecticides Fungicides	Winegrowing	Wood	Hair	Depilation				☉ SUN	☿ MERCURY	♀ VENUS	♂ MARS	♃ JUPITER	♄ SATURN	♅ URANUS	♆ NEPTUNE	♇ PLUTO
W 12	0:45 / 4:45 / 8:45 / 17:15			7:48	C		✈	🏠	✂					☉ ✱ 5	☿ 12	♀ 17					♆ 6	
T 13	2:15 / 5:45 / 9:30 / 18:15			1:10 / 8:25	C		✈	🏠											♄ 0			
F 14	3:30 / 6:45 / 10:15 / 19:30	◑		2:27 / 9:17	C		✈	🏠		/				☉ 11 △ ☿ 20						♅ 2 △	♆ 8	♇ 22
S 15	4:30 / 8:00 / 11:30 / 20:30			3:26 / 10:25	C			✗		/						♀ △ 1	♂ 3		♄ ✱ 3			
S 16	5:15 / 9:00 / 12:45 / 21:15			4:09 / 11:45	C			✗		/				☉ △ 19				♃ 4		♅ △ 6		
M 17	5:45 / 9:45 / 14:15 / 22:15			4:38 / 13:08				✗	✂	/												
T 18	6:00 / 10:45 / 15:30 / 23:00			4:58 / 14:30				✗	✂	/											♆ 19	
W 19	6:15 / 11:30 / 16:45 / 23:45	☋ 3:00		5:14 / 15:50				✗		/					☿ 20		♂ ✱ 18		♄ 14			♇ △ 9
T 20	6:30 / 12:15 / 18:00			5:27 / 17:06				✗	✂	/						♀ 0		♃ △ 18		♅ 19		
F 21	0:30 / 6:45 / 12:45 / 19:15	○		5:38 / 18:20	C			✗	✂	/				☉ 19								♇ 18

APRIL

| | | | | | | | | | | | | | | | | | | | | | | | | | |

S 12
4:15 / 7:45 / 11:30 / 20:15
3:08 / 10:34
C
☉ 20 ☿ 12 | ♂ ☌ 7 ♃ ☌ 16 | ♅ △ 15

S 13
4:45 / 8:45 / 13:00 / 21:15
3:41 / 11:57

M 14
5:00 / 9:30 / 14:15 / 22:00
4:04 / 13:19
♀ △ 1

T 15
5:15 / 10:30 / 15:45 / 22:45
4:21 / 14:38
☉ △ 6 ☿ △ 3 | ♄ ☌ 18 | ♆ ☌ 3 ♅ △ 16
♉ 7:00

W 16
5:30 / 11:00 / 17:00 / 23:30
4:35 / 15:54

T 17
5:45 / 11:45 / 18:15
4:46 / 17:08
C
♂ ✳ 1 ♃ △ 7 | ♅ ☌ 5
♉ ♃ 17:00

F 18
0:15 / 6:00 / 12:30 / 19:15
4:58 / 18:20
C
♉ 1

S 19
0:45 / 6:15 / 13:15 / 20:30
5:09 / 19:33
C
♀ ☌ 6 ♂ 13 ♃ 18 | ♆ △ 22

S 20
1:30 / 6:15 / 14:00 / 21:45
5:22 / 20:46
C F
♀ ☌ 11 ☿ ☌ 23 | ♄ ✳ 14 | ♉ ✳ 12
♌ ☿ 2:00

M 21
2:15 / 6:45 / 14:45 / 23:00
5:38 / 22:00
I

T 22
3:00 / 7:00 / 15:30
5:58 / 23:11
I
♂ △ 4 ♃ ✳ 6 | ♅ △ 4 ♆ 10

MAY

		Times of the tides	Ascending and descending moon, and moon phases	Constellations (gardening)	Times of moon rising and setting	Compost	Insecticides Fungicides	Winegrowing	Wood	Hair	Depilation				☉ SUN	☿ MERCURY	♀ VENUS	♂ MARS	♃ JUPITER	♄ SATURN	♅ URANUS	♆ NEPTUNE	♇ PLUTO
W 14		4:00 9:45 16:00 22:15			2:54 14:59										☉ △18	☿ 0	♀ △3		♃ △14		♅ ☍13		
T 15		4:00 10:30 17:15 22:45			3:06 16:11	C												♂ ✳11					♇ 6
F 16		4:15 11:15 18:30 23:30			3:17 17:23	C										☿ △15							
S 17		4:30 12:00 19:30			3:30 18:35	C													♃ 1	♄ ✳20		♆ △4	♇ ✳17
S 18		0:15 4:45 12:30 20:45			3:45 19:48	C												♂ 1					
M 19		1:00 5:00 13:30 22:00			4:04 21:00	C											♀ ☍15		♃ ✳13		♅ △12	♆ 17	
T 20		1:45 5:30 14:15 23:15	○ A15:00		4:28 22:08		F								☉ ☍3			♂ △16		♄ 8			
W 21		2:30 6:00 15:00			5:02 23:07											☿ ☍22							
T 22		0:00 3:30 6:45 16:00			5:48 23:55		F													♄ △21	♅ 1	♆ ✳5	♇ 18
F 23		1:00 4:15 7:45 16:45			6:46		F																

93

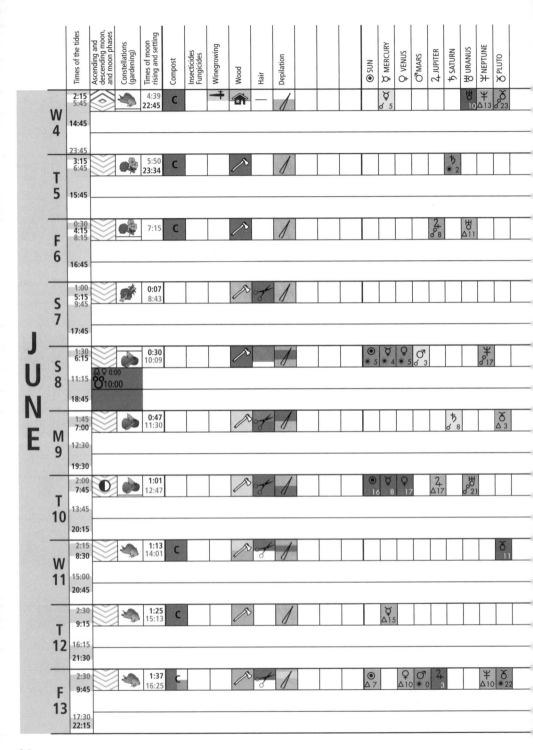

		Times of the tides	Ascending and descending moon, and moon phases	Constellations (gardening)	Times of moon rising and setting	Compost	Insecticides Fungicides	Winegrowing	Wood	Hair	Depilation				☉ SUN	☿ MERCURY	♀ VENUS	♂ MARS	♃ JUPITER	♄ SATURN	♅ URANUS	♆ NEPTUNE	♇ PLUTO
W 4		2:15 5:45 14:45 23:45			4:39 22:45	C		✝	🏠	—	/					☌ ☿ 5					☿ 10 △13 ☌ 23		
T 5		3:15 6:45 15:45			5:50 23:34	C			🪓		/									♄ ✳ 2			
F 6		0:30 4:15 8:15 16:45			7:15	C			🪓		/								♃ ☌ 8		♅ △11	
S 7		1:00 5:15 9:45 17:45			0:07 8:43				🪓 ✂		/											
S 8		1:30 6:15 11:15 18:45			0:30 10:09				🪓		/			☌ ♀ 0:00 ☊☋ 10:00	☉ ✳ 5	☿ ✳ 4	♀ ✳ 5	♂ ☌ 3				♆ ☌ 17	
M 9		1:45 7:00 12:30 19:30			0:47 11:30				🪓 ✂		/									♄ ☌ 8			♇ △ 3
T 10		2:00 7:45 13:45 20:15	◑		1:01 12:47				🪓 ✂		/				☉ 16	☿ 8	♀ 17		♃ △17		♅ ☌ 21		
W 11		2:15 8:30 15:00 20:45			1:13 14:01	C			🪓	✂	/												♇ 11
T 12		2:30 9:15 16:15 21:30			1:25 15:13	C			🪓		/					☿ △15							
F 13		2:30 9:45 17:30 22:15			1:37 16:25	C			🪓 ✂		/				☉ △ 7		♀ △10	♂ ✳ 0	♃ 3			♆ △10	♇ ✳22

JUNE

94

		Times of the tides	Ascending and descending moon, and moon phases	Constellations (gardening)	Times of moon rising and setting	Compost	Insecticides Fungicides	Winegrowing	Wood	Hair	Depilation			☉ SUN	☿ MERCURY	♀ VENUS	♂ MARS	♃ JUPITER	♄ SATURN	♅ URANUS	♆ NEPTUNE	♇ PLUTO
	W 25	1:15 7:00 13:00 19:15			0:09 12:01	C	I	🍷	🏠									♃ ✳8		♅ ♂15		
	T 26	1:15 7:45 14:15 20:00	◑		0:21 13:20			🍷						☉ 13	♀ 22						♇ 3
J U N E	F 27	1:30 8:30 15:45 21:00			0:35 14:42			🍷							☿ ✳7			♃ 13			♆ ✳22	
	S 28	1:45 9:15 17:15 21:45			0:51 16:08		F	🍷	🏠	✂				☉ ✳20			♂ △4		♄ △15			♇ △7
	S 29	2:15 10:15 18:45 22:45			1:11 17:38		F	🍷	🏠	✂						♀ ✳6		♃ △15		♅ ✳21	♆ 23	
	M 30	2:45 11:15 20:00 23:45			1:40 19:07	C	I F		🏠		/						♂ 8		♄ 16			
J U L Y	T 1	3:15 12:15 21:30			2:22 20:24	C	I	🍷	🏠				P22:00				☿ ♂15			♅ 21	♆ △23	
	W 2	1:00 4:30 13:30 22:30			3:23 21:23	C	I F	🍷		🔨	–	/						♂ ✳10		♄ ✳16			♇ ♂8
	T 3	2:00 5:45 14:30 23:00	●		4:42 22:03	C				🔨	–	/		☉ ♂3		♀ ♂15		♃ ♂14		♅ △21		
	F 4	3:00 7:15 15:30 23:30			6:11 22:31				🏠	🔨	–	/										

AUGUST

Day	Times of the tides	Ascending and descending moon, and moon phases	Constellations (gardening)	Times of moon rising and setting	Compost	Insecticides Fungicides	Winegrowing	Wood	Hair	Depilation	☉ SUN	☿ MERCURY	♀ VENUS	♂ MARS	♃ JUPITER	♄ SATURN	♅ URANUS	♆ NEPTUNE	♇ PLUTO
W 6	5:45 / 13:00 / 18:00 / 23:00			11:54 22:03	C			⚒		/	☉ ✳6				♃ 6			♆ △23	
T 7	6:30 / 14:15 / 18:45 / 23:15			13:09 22:18	C			⚒		/		☿ ✳0	♀ ✳16						♇ ✳10
F 8	7:15 / 15:30 / 19:30 / 23:30	◑		14:23 22:37	C			⚒		/	☉ 21				♃ ✳16	♄ ✳5		♆ △23	
S 9	8:00 / 16:30 / 20:15			15:35 23:02	C			⚒		/		☿ 22		♂ ✳11			♅ △8	♆ 10	
S 10	0:00 / 8:45 / 17:45 / 21:15	A 21:00		16:43 23:36				⚒		/			♀ 11			♄ 18			
M 11	0:30 / 9:30 / 18:45 / 22:00			17:43				⚒		/	☉ △15						♅ 20	♆ ✳23	
T 12	1:15 / 10:30 / 19:30 / 23:00			0:22 18:31	C	✝	✂					☿ △21		♂ 3					♇ 10
W 13	2:15 / 11:15 / 20:15 / 23:45			1:20 19:08		✝							♀ △6		♃ 16	♄ △7			
T 14	3:30 / 12:15 / 20:30			2:29 19:35		✝								♂ △18			♅ ✳8		
F 15	0:30 / 4:45 / 13:00 / 21:00			3:44 19:55	C	✝ 🏠													

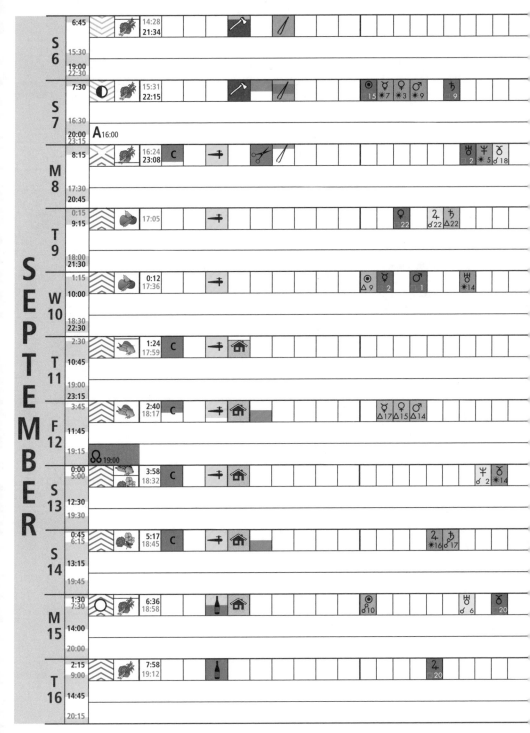

S
E
P
T
E
M
B
E
R

103

105

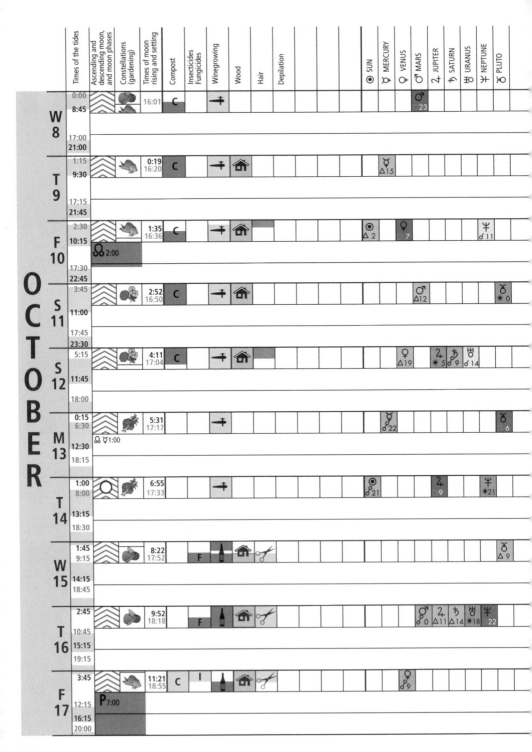

OCTOBER

		Times of the tides	Ascending and descending moon, and moon phases	Constellations (gardening)	Times of moon rising and setting	Compost	Insecticides Fungicides	Winegrowing	Wood	Hair	Depilation					☉ SUN	☿ MERCURY	♀ VENUS	♂ MARS	♃ JUPITER	♄ SATURN	♅ URANUS	♆ NEPTUNE	♇ PLUTO
W 8		0:00 / 8:45			16:01	C		✚											♂ 23					
		17:00 / 21:00																						
T 9		1:15 / 9:30			0:19 / 16:20	C		✚	🏠									☿ △15						
		17:15 / 21:45																						
F 10		2:30 / 10:15	☊ 2:00		1:35 / 16:36	C		✚	🏠							☉ △ 2		♀ 7					♆ ♂ 11	
		17:30 / 22:45																						
S 11		3:45 / 11:00			2:52 / 16:50	C		✚	🏠										♂ △12					☿ ✳ 0
		17:45 / 23:30																						
S 12		5:15 / 11:45			4:11 / 17:04	C		✚	🏠									♀ △19		♃ ✳ 5 / ♄ ♂ 9 / ♅ ♂ 14				
		18:00																						
M 13		0:15 / 6:30	☊ ☿ 1:00		5:31 / 17:17			✚										♀ ♂ 22						♂ □ 6
		12:30 / 18:15																						
T 14		1:00 / 8:00	○		6:55 / 17:33			✚								☉ ♂ 21				♃ ♂ 9			♆ ✳21	
		13:15 / 18:30																						
W 15		1:45 / 9:15			8:22 / 17:52	F		🍾	🏠	✂														♂ △ 9
		14:15 / 18:45																						
T 16		2:45 / 10:45			9:52 / 18:18	F		🍾	🏠	✂									♂ ♂ 0	♃ △11 / ♄ △14 / ♅ ✳18			♆ 22	
		15:15 / 19:15																						
F 17		3:45 / 12:15	P 7:00		11:21 / 18:55	C	I	🍾	🏠	✂								♀ ♂ 9						
		16:15 / 20:00																						

OCTOBER

Date		Times														Planets

S 18 — 4:45 / 13:45 / 17:15 / 20:45 — 12:41 / 19:46 — C — I F — 🍾 — 🏠 — ✏️ — ☿△0 — ♄ 16 — ♅ 19 — ♆△23

S 19 — 5:45 / 14:45 / 18:15 / 22:00 — 13:46 / 20:55 — C — I — 🍾 — 🪓 — ✏️ — ☉△6 — ☿ 11

M 20 — 6:45 / 15:30 / 19:15 / 23:15 — 14:32 / 22:15 — I F — 🍾 — 🪓 — ✏️ — ☿♂2:00 — 4 — ♂△7 — 2 ♂14 — ♄※18 — ♅△21

T 21 — 7:45 / 16:00 / 20:15 — 15:04 / 23:40 — I — 🍾 — 🪓 — ✏️ — ☉ 13 — ♀△22

W 22 — 0:45 / 8:45 / 16:30 / 21:15 — 15:27 — 🍾 — 🪓 — ✂️ — ✏️ — ☿※11 — ♂ 14 — ☊19:00

T 23 — 2:00 / 9:30 / 16:45 / 22:00 — 1:03 / 15:44 — 🪓 — ✂️ — ✏️ — ☉※22 — ♆♂5 — ☿△19

F 24 — 3:30 / 10:15 / 17:00 / 22:45 — 2:24 / 15:58 — F — 🍾 — 🪓 — ✂️ — ✏️ — ♀ 9 — ♂※22

S 25 — 4:45 / 11:00 / 17:15 / 23:30 — 3:41 / 16:11 — F — 🍾 — 🪓 — ✂️ — ✏️ — 2△2 — ♄♂5 — ♅☊8

S 26 — 5:00 / 10:45 / 16:30 / 23:15 — 3:57 / 15:23 — I F — 🍾 — 🪓 — ✂️ — ✏️ — ♀※21 — ☿ 2

M 27 — 6:15 / 11:30 / 16:30 — 5:12 / 15:37 — I F — 🍾 — 🪓 — ✏️ — ☿♂12 — 2 9 — ♆△19

T 28 — 0:00 / 7:30 / 12:15 / 16:45 — 6:27 / 15:52 — C — I — 🍾 — 🪓 — — — ✏️ — ☉♂23 — ☿※10

Date	Times of the tides	Moon phase / Asc-Desc	Constellation	Moon rising and setting	Compost	Insecticides/Fungicides	Winegrowing	Wood	Hair	Depilation	Planetary aspects
W 29	0:45 / 8:45 / 13:00 / 17:15	● (new moon)	🌱	7:42 / 16:11	C			🪓	—	✂	♂ ☌22 ♃ ✳20
T 30	1:30 / 10:00 / 13:45 / 17:30		🌱	8:55 / 16:36	C			🪓	—	✂	♄ ✳0 ♅ △1 ♆ 6
F 31	2:15 / 11:00 / 14:45 / 18:15		🌱	10:04 / 17:09				🪓		✂	
S 1	3:00 / 12:00 / 15:30 / 19:00		🌱	11:05 / 17:53				🪓		✂	♀ ☌8 ♄ 12 ♅ 13 ♆ ✳18
S 2	4:00 / 13:00 / 16:15 / 19:45	A 5:00	🌸	11:55 / 18:48		🌿			✂		☿ ✳3 ♇ ☌10
M 3	4:45 / 13:30 / 17:15 / 21:00		🌸	12:33 / 19:53		🌿					☉ ✳10 ♂ ☌22
T 4	5:30 / 14:00 / 18:00 / 22:00		🌸	13:01 / 21:03		🌿					♂ ✳7 ♄ △2 ♅ ✳2
W 5	6:15 / 14:30 / 18:45 / 23:15		🌼	13:23 / 22:16	C	🌿	🏠				♀ □1
T 6	7:00 / 14:45 / 19:30	◑ (first quarter); ☊ 4:00	🌼	13:40 / 23:31	C		🏠				☉ 4 ♀ ✳22 ♂ 22 ♆ ☌18
F 7	0:30 / 7:45 / 15:00 / 20:15		🌱	13:55	C	🌿	🏠				☿ △20 ♇ ✳10
S 8	1:45 / 8:30 / 15:15 / 21:00		🌱	0:46 / 14:08	C	🌿	🏠				☉ △18 ♃ ✳20 ♄ ☌23 ♅ ☌22
S 9	3:00 / 9:15 / 15:15 / 21:45		🦀	2:04 / 14:21		🌿	🏠				♀ 11 ♂ △9 ♇ 16
M 10	4:30 / 10:00 / 15:30 / 22:30		🦀	3:24 / 14:36		🌿					
T 11	5:45 / 11:00 / 16:00 / 23:30		🌿	4:48 / 14:53	C	🌿					♀ △18 ♃ 1 ♆ ✳6 ♇ △19
W 12	7:15 / 12:00 / 16:15		🌹	6:17 / 15:16		🌿	🏠 ✂				☿ ☌17

Column headers (full): Times of the tides · Ascending and descending moon, and moon phases · Constellations (gardening) · Times of moon rising and setting · Compost · Insecticides Fungicides · Winegrowing · Wood · Hair · Depilation · ☉ SUN · ☿ MERCURY · ♀ VENUS · ♂ MARS · ♃ JUPITER · ♄ SATURN · ♅ URANUS · ♆ NEPTUNE · ♇ PLUTO

DECEMBER

Date	Times of the tides	Ascending/descending moon, and moon phases	Constellations (gardening)	Times of moon rising and setting	Compost	Insecticides Fungicides	Winegrowing	Wood	Hair	Depilation	SUN ☉	MERCURY ☿	VENUS ♀	MARS ♂	JUPITER ♃	SATURN ♄	URANUS ♅	NEPTUNE ♆	PLUTO ♇
S 30	2:45 / 11:30 / 15:00 / 18:45			10:31 / 17:43			✈												
M 1	3:30 / 12:00 / 16:00 / 19:45			11:03 / 18:52			✈						♂16		♂15	△12	✳8		
T 2	4:15 / 12:30 / 16:45 / 21:00			11:26 / 20:04	C		✈	🏠											
W 3	5:00 / 12:45 / 17:30 / 22:15	☊ 5:00		11:45 / 21:16	C		✈	🏠			✳6	✳15		✳7					
T 4	5:45 / 13:00 / 18:15 / 23:30			12:00 / 22:30	C		✈	🏠										♂2	✳19
F 5	6:30 / 13:15 / 18:45	◑		12:13 / 23:43	C		✈	🏠			21			21					
S 6	0:45 / 7:15 / 13:30 / 19:30			12:26	C		✈	🏠				9			✳15	♂11	♂6		
S 7	2:00 / 8:00 / 13:45 / 20:15			0:59 / 12:39			✈						✳1						3
M 8	3:15 / 8:45 / 14:00 / 21:15			2:19 / 12:54			✈				△8	△22		△7	20			✳17	
T 9	4:45 / 9:30 / 14:15 / 22:00			3:43 / 13:14			✈	🏠	✂				10						△8
W 10	6:15 / 10:30 / 14:45 / 23:00			5:12 / 13:40			✈	🏠	✂						△22	△18	✳14	19	
T 11	7:45 / 11:30 / 15:15			6:41 / 14:18	C		✈	🏠					△14						
F 12	0:00 / 9:00 / 12:45 / 16:15	○		8:04 / 15:14	C		✈	🏠			♂17			♂13		17	13	△18	
S 13	P 22:00 / 1:15 / 10:15 / 13:45 / 17:30			9:10 / 16:28	C I		🍾	🔨	/			♂9							✳8
S 14	2:15 / 11:00 / 14:45 / 19:00			9:57 / 17:56		I / F	🍾	🔨	/						♂23	✳18	△13		

111

Plan of your garden

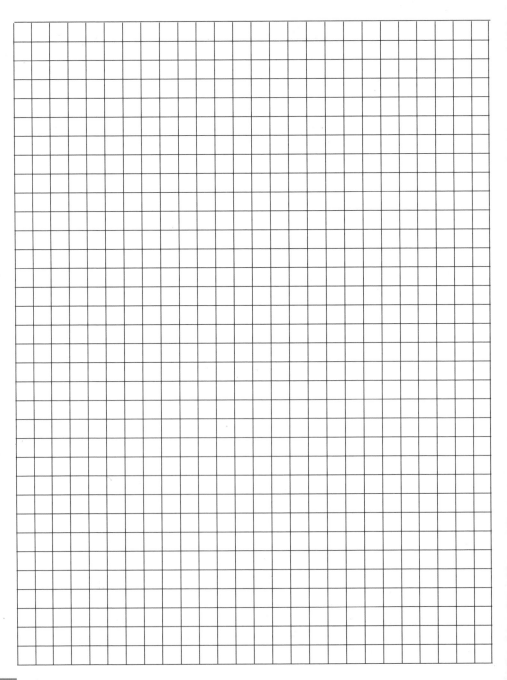